MOZART

his life and times

MOZART

his life and times

E. S. Tchernaya
Translated from the Russian by Yuri Sviridov

General Editor
Dr. Mark Zilberquit

ISBN 0-86622-332-0

TFH PUBLICATIONS, INC.
211 West Sylvania Avenue
Neptune City, NJ 07753

B
MOZART

Contents

Introduction

More than two hundred years have passed since the birth of Wolfgang Amadeus Mozart but time has not diminished the greatness and beauty of his compositions. His symphonies and concertos can be heard in every concert hall, his operas are produced by the world's best opera houses, his serenades, songs and chamber compositions are the music for an intimate hour, while to this day, his masses and requiems soar to the vaulted heights of churches and cathedrals. Mozart's work lives on; indeed today, after a lapse of two centuries, Mozart is nearer to us than he was to his own world of the Viennese Court and Viennese society, which did not give him the recognition due to his unique genius. Mozart is also nearer to us today than to the world of a hundred years ago when, at his centennial, doubts were expressed by some experts as to whether his work was really so great. Today Mozart is among the immortals of this world.

For over two centuries, Mozart's personality and fate have stirred the imagination of poets, musicians and scholars. The extraordinarily early flowering of his genius, its universality, the remarkable and apparently inexplicable ease with which he composed and his untimely death, have all made him legend in the eyes of his contemporaries and posterity alike. Much time had to pass before the poetic myth was dispelled to reveal the true picture of this courageous, hardworking and bold artist, extolled and yet unappreciated by his contemporaries who encompassed his ruin.

Mozart died before reaching the age of thirty-six but during his short life his art achieved a maturity usually associated with long experience of life. Crowning the achievements of 18th-century music, it opened up new vistas for the artists of succeeding generations. Mozart's works were regarded as a source of the highest inspiration, perfection and musical truth by his senior, Haydn, and by Beethoven, Schubert and such dissimilar composers of other countries as Rossini, Mendelssohn, Chopin, Gounod, Grieg, Glinka, Tchaikovsky and many others.

Mozart had a rare gift for blending the beautiful in art with a profound understanding of life, and directness of temperament with an indomitable will and the courage of firm convictions.

His was the work of a man of action struggling for his own happiness, suffering, reflecting, or overcome with passion. Mozart studied with keen attention the characters and relationships of the people around him, their day-to-day conflicts and their lofty aspirations. This comprehensive psychological perception was reflected in the inexhaustible wealth and generosity of his means of expression; perfect mastery in writing for the human voice and no less perfect mastery of the orchestra meant that in Mozart's operas the parts of singers and instrumentalists were equally expressive.

But for Mozart, no instrument could replace the inspired sound of the human voice; the converse, rather. All his instrumental works acquired the cadences of human speech. His musical imagery comes over to the listener as something whole, something integral that never loses the appeal of close and direct contact with reality. That is one reason why Mozart's works are immortal.

Chapter 1

Childhood and Prodigy Years

Wolfgang Amadeus Mozart was born at Salzburg, then a prince-archbishopric of the Holy Roman Empire, on 27 January, 1756. According to the baptismal register of the Salzburg Cathedral for 1756 he was baptized Joannes Chrysostomus Wolfgangus Theophilus Mozart on January 28. To his family he was always Wolfgang.

Mozart's birthplace. A drawing. (Schenk, *Mozart and His Times*).

The room in which Mozart was born. The Mozart house was acquired by the International Foundation of the Mozarteum in 1917, and is now a notable museum.

Perhaps no other composer has owed as much to Mother Nature and his own father as Mozart. He came into the world endowed with a natural gift unprecedented in the history of music, and it was his good fortune to have a father who was able to develop his native genius and groom him to musical greatness. Leopold Mozart, Wolfgang's father, was a native of Augsburg, where he was born on November 14, 1719, the son of a bookbinder. From an early age he had ambition and determination. His musical education began in a monastery where he learned to play the violin and the organ. For a time he intended to train for the priesthood but when he entered the University of Salzburg it was logic and law rather than theology that attracted him most. Music, however, was his first love and proved to be his prime concern. A violinist of some note, he became musician and chamberlain to Count Thurn and Taxis, Canon of Salzburg, and later joined the private orchestra of the Archbishop of Salzburg.

Leopold was well-grounded in composition and wrote religious music, also symphonies, concertos, and clavier sonatas. Aside from being the father of his illustrious son, however, his main claim to fame is his *Versuch einen Grundlichen Violinschule* (Augsburg, 1756) which went through many editions in several

Salzburg, with the Archbishop's palace, the Cathedral, the Nonnberg Convent and St. Peter's Monastery. A contemporary painting.

languages and was for long the authoritative method for the violin.

In 1747 Leopold Mozart married Anna Maria Pertl, daughter of an official of St. Gilgen, near Salzburg. Of seven children born to them only two survived, a daughter, Maria Anna (nicknamed Nannerl), and a son, Wolfgang. Interestingly, the elder Mozarts were spoken of as the handsomest couple in Salzburg.

Leopold was strict, pedagogic, and rather domineering in his own family, though not above servility and deference in his attitude towards station and power. Fortunately, Wolfgang who had to undergo his rigorous training was a very affectionate child and touchingly devoted to his stern father.

At a very early age both Nannerl and Wolfgang exhibited an uncommon aptitude for music and Leopold soon began to devote much of his time to the training of his gifted children. Per-

Leopold Mozart
(1719-87). Frontispiece to
the first edition of his
Violin School, 1756.

haps Leopold's true genius lay precisely in his grasping at an early stage both the creative and the commercial potential of the extraordinary precocity of his children as their extensive European concert tours showed. There was perhaps something that smacked of the showman in the way Leopold exhibited them as prodigies all over Europe and the strain of those years of travel and gruelling performances must have affected Wolfgang's health.

Even as a child of three Mozart showed an eager and intelligent interest in music. He listened to his sister's harpsichord lessons and amused himself for hours by picking out chords on the instrument. And he displayed an extraordinary memory for the pieces he heard. Encouraged by these indications his father began to teach him little minuets on the harpsichord. At five Wolfgang began to compose little imitations, his happy father carefully writing down what he invented. Those early pieces already betrayed his feeling for the beauty of sound and form.

Maria Anna ('Nannerl') Mozart (1751-1829). The superimposed head was probably done by Pietro Antonio Lorenzoni in 1763. The rest of the body and the background would have been painted beforehand as was the custom of the period. Nannerl married in 1784. On her husband's death in 1801 she devoted herself to teaching in Salzburg. Becoming blind in 1820, she died in poverty.

Before long Wolfgang was able to enter his own compositions in the music-book.

Regular coaching began when Wolfgang was four, Leopold moving cautiously so as not to put an undue strain on the boy. But it seemed that no piece was too difficult for Wolfgang. He was endowed with a splendid pair of hands for playing, and was well equipped for every technical difficulty. His extraordinarily retentive memory enabled him to memorise instantly everything he heard while the inborn dexterity of his fingers helped Wolfgang to cope with the most complex clavier pieces.

The manuscript music-book compiled by Leopold for his little prodigies contains this entry made within a few months of regular teaching for his son: "Wolfgang learned this minuet in

German clavichord, 1763.

Harpsichord by Johann Adolf Hass of Hamburg, 1764. The instrument was restored in about 1840, which may explain why the natural keys are ivory and the accidentals ebony: normally these colours would have been reversed, with ebony natural keys and ivory accidentals. This instrument appears to have once belonged to Mozart himself. (Russell Collection, University of Edinburgh).

14

Mozart in 1762 at the age of six. He is seen wearing a court suit originally intended for the Archduke Maximilian and given to him by the Empress Maria Theresa. The painting has been attributed to Pietro Antonio Lorenzoni.

half an hour at ten in the evening on the eve of his fifth birthday." There are even earlier entries in a similar vein. Once, when he was just four, Wolfgang wrote down a harpsichord concerto. When Leopold commented jokingly that it would be impossible to perform Wolfgang took umbrage and said that any concerto had to be rehearsed carefully and for some little time.

For the rest, aside from his phenomenal musical talents, Wolfgang was a child like any other: playful, exuberantly cheerful, naughty at times, and very communicative. His music lessons were to him a natural part of his life, and like any other pastime to which Wolfgang devoted himself wholeheartedly, great fun.

By age six Wolfgang had mastered harpsichord playing technique and somewhat later it was also discovered that quite without any formal teaching he could also play the violin and the organ.

The father, struck by the unbelievably rapid progress of his children, decided to travel with them to present his little "prodigies of nature" to the world. The thought that his exceptionally gifted son would have to follow in his footsteps was a source of constant worry to Leopold. He realised he had to gain general public recognition for Wolfgang's talents and had to do so quickly while he was still young.

He started at the top, his first venture being at the Electoral Court of Munich where he took his children in January 1762 after obtaining a leave of absence from the Archbishop of Salz-

Vienna, the Lobkowitz
Palace, residence of one
of the great Viennese
patrons of music.
Painting by Bernardo
Bellotto, a nephew of
Canaletto, about 1760.

Austrian pedal grand piano,
probably by Johann
Schmidt, late 18th century.
Leopold Mozart
recommended Schmidt to
the Salzburg court and
Wolfgang must have been
familiar with his
instruments
(Nürnberg, Rück
Collection, Germanisches
Nationalmuseum).

Carl Theodor, Elector
Palatine (1742-1799).

burg. The Elector Carl Theodor received them kindly and expressed admiration. Even so they seemed to have made less of an impact at Munich than Leopold had hoped for. But nothing could dampen his determination now. Encouraged by the initial success in the Bavarian capital Leopold went to Vienna—his next port of call.

The reputation of the little prodigies had preceded them to the capital. But the reality exceeded by far and away the expectations of the court and nobility. In Vienna everything that Leopold could have possibly wished happened.

Their appearance in Vienna caused a sensation. Upon arrival Leopold was informed that he had been granted the privilege of presenting his astonishing children at court. For two weeks the Emperor and his family, at Schonbrunn Palace, their summer residence, enjoyed the marvellous artistry of the two virtuosi: they played solo and ensemble, they performed pieces for four hands on the same harpsichord, and Wolfgang played improvis-

Violin used by Mozart in
his childhood.

'THEOPH: W: MOZART Compositeur.et Maitre de Musique.age de 7 ans.

Mozart, aged 7.

ations on themes set to him by his hearers, as well as his own compositions. He was asked to play clavier pieces with the keyboard covered. On one occasion in the presence of Wagenseil, the court composer, he played at sight one of his most intricate clavier concertos. Wolfgang asked expressly for Wagenseil that he might be sure of having a real connoisseur among his audience for he really cared only for the approval of connoisseurs. Wolfgang's amazing artistic freedom coupled with his naivety and ingenuous manner charmed and delighted all who heard him. He treated the Empress Maria Theresa with all the spontaneity of an unspoilt child, climbing into her lap, and kissing her. Of course, the nobility went wild about Leopold Mozart's astonishing children and all the ladies lost their hearts to the "little sprightly fellow".

But a change occurred at the end of October, when Wolfgang caught scarlet fever which laid him up for a long time.

Meanwhile Leopold's leave of absence from the Archbishop's service had expired and the family had to return to Salzburg early in 1763. But a good start had been made nonetheless and a few months later Leopold attempted a much longer journey, his prime objective this time being Paris.

On June 9, 1763 the Mozarts set out on a three-year long trip to France and England that took them through a number of South-and West-German cities—including Munich and Frank-

Salzburg. An engraving.

furt—also Belgium, Holland, south-eastern France, Switzerland, and Leopold's home city of Augsburg, giving public and private concerts and playing at many courts on the way. Wolfgang played the violin and also the organ at various churches and cathedrals.

The warm, ecstatic welcome accorded to the child prodigies at royal palaces and aristocratic salons, the general petting and patronage lavished on them by the nobility, their meetings with the leading lights of the artistic world, the steady flow of ovation and public acclaim, of praise and gifts combined to lend Mozart's childhood years a fairy-tale aureole, especially as described by those of his biographers who either unconsciously or intentionally overlooked all the darker dissonances in Mozart's life and work. The sheer number of cities in Germany, France, England, Holland and Switzerland where Mozart and Nannerl had to give concerts and exhibition performances gives an idea of the tremendous physical and psychological strain imposed on the prodigies and makes one realise what a harsh school of professional life those trips were.

On the way to Paris the pair gave concerts in many German cities, and in the various castles and country residences where the aristocracy repaired for the summer. Their fame preceded their arrival wherever they went, while their concerts were given loud advance publicity which emphasised their extraordinary gifts. Here is a typical announcement of a public concert in Frankfurt: "Today, Wednesday August 30, the last concert will be given at 6 p.m.: a girl of twelve and a boy of seven will play a number of concertos for harpsichord and clavier, with the former performing some of the most difficult works of the old masters. Besides, the boy will play a violin concerto, will accompany the performance of a symphony on the harpsichord, and also play with the keyboard covered as freely as he would with the keyboard before his eyes. Later he will also identify, at a distance, the names of all the sounds to be played to him singly or as chords on the harpsichord or any other instrument, or will be produced by various objects such as a bell, a glass or a clock. Finally, the boy will play improvisations both on the harpsichord and on the organ for as long as the audience would care to listen and in the most difficult tonalities set to him in order to show that he is equally at home on the organ which, of course, is a very different instrument from the harpsichord."

In those days a typical concert would last four to five hours, a tough marathon even for experienced adult performers. Leopold had no option but to proceed with the concert tour for nothing short of sensational performances by his astonishing children could yield a financial return large enough to cover the travel expenses.

Detail of the illustration below showing Mozart at the clavier.

Mozart playing at a musical tea at the Prince de Conti's town house in Paris, 1764.

Leopold Mozart with
Wolfgang and Nannerl in
Paris. Watercolour by
Carmontelle, 1763.
Delafosse subsequently
made an engraving of this
picture which was then
used as the basis for an
advertisement distributed
throughout Europe (Musée
Condé, Chantilly).

Mozart and his sister, about 1763.

Leopold Mozart, about 1763.

Friedrich Melchior Grimm (1723-1807), friend of Diderot and Rousseau and founder of the famous *Correspondance littéraire.* Watercolour by Carmontelle, 1778 (Musée Condé, Chantilly).

At a concert in Frankfurt Goethe first heard Mozart. The great poet recalled later: "I was about fourteen, and I still distinctly remember the little man with his frizzled wig, and sword." Indeed the children's appearance at those concerts was most memorable as they were dressed in the heavy goldbraid court uniforms presented to them by the royal family in Vienna.

The Mozarts arrived in Paris on November 18, 1764 carrying a letter of recommendation secured on the way and called on Baron Grimm, the outstanding French journalist and critic who shared the liberal ideas of the Encyclopedists. Melchior Grimm took them up warmly and was of great use in obtaining introductions for them and rendering services of various kinds. As a result, the Mozarts were invited to appear at court where Nannerl and Wolfgang played before Louis XV's family at Versailles, and gave two concerts which generated tremendous enthusiam. The Emperor's daughters were delighted by the children.

Through Baron Grimm's good offices the Mozarts were soon drawn into the heady excitement and glitter of the social whirlpool of Paris, the most cosmopolitan of European metropolises at the time. Concerts followed in the palaces of the aristocracy. The ambassadors of England and of Russia showed great interest.

The atmosphere of social life in Paris could not have been more different from that of Vienna, let alone Salzburg. The acrimonious polemic over social issues in the journals and in the

Marie Leszcynska, Queen of France.

Title page of Mozart's first published work.

Versailles, the palace and gardens.

Louis XV (1710-74). Portrait by Louis-Michel Vanloo (Grenoble Museum).

Paris in the 18th century.

King George III of England (1737-1820).

Title page of the sonatas dedicated
to Queen Charlotte.

Six
SONATES
pour le
CLAVECIN
qui peuvent se jouer avec
L'accompagnement de Violon ou Flaute
Traversiere
Tres humblement dediées
A SA MAJESTÉ
CHARLOTTE
REINE de la GRANDE BRETAGNE
Composées par
I.G. WOLFGANG MOZART
Agé de huit Ans
Oeuvre III.

LONDON Printed for the author and Sold at his Lodging
at Mr Williamson in Thrift Street Soho.

Queen Charlotte of England (1744-1818). She married George III in 1761 and bore him fifteen children.

press, the freedom and unrestricted range of philosophical views expressed on all sides and the controversy they generated added up to a liberal's paradise as compared to the relatively cloistered, slow-moving world of German and Austrian cities. In the quality and standard of artistic life even glittering Vienna looked provincial beside Paris.

At Versailles the Mozarts heard first-class choral and church music. France had long enjoyed a high standard of choral singing and organ music. It also possessed a supremely disciplined symphony orchestra made up of some of Europe's best musicians. From the days of Lulli on this orchestra had been preeminent in Europe and its concerts, whose programmes included the latest symphonic works by outstanding French and foreign composers, invariably attracted a wide range of music lovers and connoisseurs.

Theatrical life in Paris was even more intensive and vibrant. The old-established royal opera house which staged the lyrical tragedies of Rameau and Lulli was in the middle of a tug-of-war with the new genre of *l'opera comique* (comic opera) which having originated as popular musical entertainment at fairs was now struggling for its share of popularity and recognition relying on its new and rapidly expanding democratic audience. Against the backdrop of this dynamic concert and theatrical life with its new progressive ideas the aristocratic salons stuck to their traditions and continued to hold elaborate concerts of chamber music dominated by harpsichord and ensemble pieces. It was at one such concert that Wolfgang heard Schobert, an outstanding harpsichord player and composer and came under his influence. Evidence of this influence was provided later by the six sonatas Mozart dedicated to the English Queen Charlotte in January 1765. A Silesian by birth, Schobert had for some years made his home in Paris. His music exhibited a passionate temperament, was full of inner dramatism and made a deep impression on the young Mozart.

For six months the astonishing children were the central attraction of Paris's aristocratic salons and, as in Vienna, were the object of adulation at court. On New Year's eve they were even allowed to stand next to the king's table which was regarded as a special honour at the time.

In Paris, Wolfgang did a little composing, producing his first four sonatas for harpsichord and violin. The father had them published in January 1765. After two brilliantly successful public concerts in April Leopold Mozart, considering his conquest of Paris complete, moved on to London.

They arrived in London on April 22, 1764 and took lodgings in Cecil Court, St. Martin's Lane. In the English capital, too,

The Inside View of the Rotunda in Ranelagh Gardens, with the Company at Breakfast. An engraving, 1754. At this renowned place of 18th century London Mozart appeared at a charity concert at the age of eight years.

The great Florentine castrato, Giovanni Manzuoli (1725-80). Engraving by G.B. Betti after the portrait by Luigi Betti.

they received a most gracious welcome at court and Wolfgang especially, made an extraordinary impression. King George III and Queen Charlotte, both of whom were musical, received them cordially and without ceremony. The king set before the "invincible" Wolfgang difficult pieces by contemporary composers: J. C. Bach, Able, Wagenseil and Handel which he played at sight with perfect ease. Wolfgang then played accompaniments for the Queen and her flutist and then extemporised a melody to the bass part of one of Handel's airs.

The really important consequences, however, of the fifteen months in England were Wolfgang's meeting with three musicians of note—Carl Friedrich Abel, a composer who had been a pupil of Johann Sebastian Bach; Sebastian's youngest son, Johann Christian, who at twenty-nine was enjoying great favour at court as an operatic composer besides being music-master to the Queen. The third was the opera singer Manzuoli who gave him singing lessons of his own accord.

Although Abel influenced Wolfgang in the initial part of his stay in London, more profound and further-reaching was Wolfgang's friendship with Christian Bach.

Indeed, the influence of this composer who, apart from his genuine interest in the child prodigy from Salzburg, treated him with something approaching tenderness, came to be for some time the dominant factor in Wolfgang's musical development. Although Christian Bach's music had nothing left of the austere polyphonic style of his great father, the caressing enchanting melodies which permeated his sonatas and concertos and the sensual charm and grace of his arias represented that easy and "sweet" style which, having originated in Italy, was now conquering the whole of Europe. The radiant joyous elements of Christian Bach's work, the melodic fullness and flexibility of his compositions impressed the young Mozart deeply.

Quite different was the contribution made by Manzuoli to Mozart's musical evolution. A musician of supreme accomplishment and a vocal virtuoso, he gave Wolfgang singing lessons free and it can safely be said that Mozart's early mastery of the secrets of writing for the human voice can be attributed to Manzuoli's instruction.

Little by little composition became a prime interest for Wolfgang, the focus of his musical creativity. To composition he devoted all his spare time writing pieces for harpsichord and violin and also trying his hand at the symphony.

While in England he received his first introduction to vocal music and vocal technique. Leopold made a point of showing Wolfgang Italian opera anticipating the role it would come to play in his son's future career. Thus it was that while Wolfgang

London and the Thames in 1750.

St. James's Park and Buckingham House, London. An engraving, 1763.

Two views of Chelsea.

Manuscript of Mozart's motet "God is our refuge," written in England.

The 1764 'Chelsea Notebook.' A facsimile of bars 18-36 of the thirty-fourth piece. The manuscript, originally in the Preussische Staatsbibliothek, Berlin, has been lost since the Second World War.

had arrived in England as essentially a virtuoso he was leaving it as a composer in his own right. During the Mozarts' sojourn in London he wrote six new sonatas for harpsichord and violin which were published. Two symphonies were written independently during his father's illness.

Not being able to play any instrument for fear of disturbing his father Wolfgang composed his first two symphonies and amused himself with experiments in composition which are of special interest in that they were never intended for his father's eyes and for this reason were never corrected by him. He also wrote 43 pieces for clavier including dances, rondos and parts of various sonatas.

From England the Mozarts went to Holland.

They arrived at the Hague in the middle of September and were most graciously received by the Prince of Orange. A concert was announced for September 30 but on the eve of the concert Nannerl fell ill and then Wolfgang developed a violent fever which lasted for weeks. Both needed a long rest.

It was not until January 1766 then that the Mozarts were able to proceed to Amsterdam where they gave two public concerts. In March they went back to the Hague for the festivities on the occasion of the installation of the Prince of Orange, for which Wolfgang composed harpsichord variations on an air by Graaf and on a Dutch folksong (now the Dutch national anthem) which were immediately engraved.

In spite of illnesses of one or the other of the children the tour continued in triumph taking them from Holland to Paris again, to Switzerland for the first time. Leopold's leave of absence had, in the meantime, long expired and although it flattered the Archbishop's self-esteem to know that his "servants" had gained European renown he began to express his displeasure.

The Mozarts started on the return journey to Salzburg giving, as usual, many concerts on the way. On 9 July they left Paris and travelling via Dijon and Lyons arrived in Switzerland where they spent many a pleasant day in Geneva, Lausanne, Berne and Zurich. The Mozarts were feted everywhere but most of all in Zurich where the poet Gessner was a most cordial and hospitable host.

Travelling further through Germany they gave concerts in the palatial residences of various German princes.

Passing through Munich on the last leg of their homeward

The residence of the Stadtholder in The Hague. An engraving.

36

Munich, the
Nymphenburg Castle.
Engraving by Jungwirth,
1766.

journey they played before the Elector, who was much pleased with Wolfgang's progress and asked the Mozarts to dinner. The travellers returned to Salzburg in November 1766.

For three years Wolfgang had been away from home. He had grown homesick and it seemed to him that there was nothing in the whole wide world like his quiet home town cradled in a mountainous setting of breathtaking beauty. He was overjoyed to meet his friends on his return. The neighbours observed him with curious interest and found that he had remained his ingenuous sprightly self; he still enjoyed playing with his toys and engaged in some horse-play with their children between music lessons.

Upon their return to Salzburg Leopold's first priority was to resume his son's interrupted studies. The subsequent months were for Wolfgang a period of unremitting study and active composing and arranging. The father who saw better than anyone the gaps in his son's musical education worked hard to eliminate them. Apparently, Leopold also directed Wolfgang's general education for there is no evidence that Wolfgang ever attended school. People who knew him as a child remarked that

Maximilian III, Elector
of Bavaria.

he showed excellent ability for mathematics. He also had a gift
for languages, too, gaining a good command of Latin, Italian, a
language essential for a musician, French and English.

Incidentally, shortly after their return to Salzburg, the Archbishop, skeptical of Wolfgang's powers, had him kept in isolation for a week in order to test his independent ability as a composer. Later he gave him the first part of a sacred cantata to
compose under strict supervision. The work was performed in
the spring of 1767 by the students in the Salzburg University
hall. Wolfgang also wrote his first little opera, a Latin comedy,
"*Appollo et Hyacinthus*" (Appollo and Hyacinth) whose music
showed how important the Salzburg baroque tradition was to
the young Mozart's development. To this period also belong a
series of virtuoso arrangements in the form of pianoforte concertos of movements from three harpsichord sonatas by Christian Bach, Schobert and other contemporary composers. Wolfgang arranged them for harpsichord and orchestra as part of
preparations for his next concert tour.

In early September 1767 Vienna was looking forward to the excitement of yet another round of court festivities—the betrothal of the Archduchess Maria Josepha and the King of Naples. Leopold Mozart, seeing this as a favourable opportunity, went to Vienna with his family. But they came in for a series of misfortunes. There was an outbreak of smallpox in Vienna and the Archduchess died of it. The nobility fled the capital fearing infection and the Mozarts too went to the neighbouring town of Olmutz where, nevertheless, both Nannerl and Wolfgang came down with the smallpox and for nine days Wolfgang was blind.

After their recovery they made a short visit to Brno where they were kindly received by Count Schrantenbach and other nobles.

When Leopold and his astonishing children returned to Vienna in January 1768 concert soirees, elaborate expensive affairs, were no longer in vogue having been supplanted by the latest enthusiasm for public balls.

Despite the assistance of a number of highly-placed friends no public concerts could be arranged for the Mozarts. Only the Russian ambassador, Prince Golitsyn, was eager and generous enough to fete them at a private concert given in their honour.

In spite of some disappointments and difficulties the trip to Vienna had a positive effect on Wolfgang's subsequent development for here he obtained his first commission to write an opera. That was the fulfilment of his father's long-cherished dream. Leopold was realistic enough to see that adult musicians now saw his twelve-year-old son not only as a boy prodigy but also as a dangerous rival. Worse than everything else was the envy and jealousy shown by court musicians. In the midst of various difficulties, however, the Emperor commissioned Wolfgang to compose an opera and conduct it at the harpsichord. Envy and professional intrigues, something that the thirteen-year-old Mozart had no idea of, were now being displayed quite openly. New and convincing proof of Wolfgang's unique genius was needed, one that would conquer all and rekindle the former sensational interest in his prodigious talents.

The boy set to work with great enthusiasm. *La Finta semplice* (The Pretended Simpleton), an *opera buffa*, was chosen on a libretto by Carlo Goldoni as adapted by Marco Coltellini. The thirteen-year-old Wolfgang composed a series of musical set pieces for this, his first comic opera. Certain arias, especially those given to Donna Giacinta, the heroine, have a sentimental tone, suggesting that Mozart might have been familiar with some of the music written by Giovanni Paisiello, a composer who introduced the sentimental into *opera buffa*. At the time Italian comic opera had gained great popularity throughout Europe. A simple straightforward plot, life-like characters, dynamic action, the light and vivacious music score had combined to assure its rapid spread. Vienna had a first-class Italian troupe who specialised in *opera buffa* and it was their high standards that the young Mozart set out to meet when he worked on *La Finta semplice*.

As he progressed the boy showed completed parts to members of the future cast who marvelled at his knowledge of all the secrets of writing for the human voice. Wolfgang was most accommodating in changing the individual parts at the request of the singers to fit them to their vocal range and preferences. It seemed Wolfgang was well on the road to a brilliant success. But it was not to be. A series of intrigues prevented the production of the opera. Apparently the management of the royal opera house had their own economic motives and calculations to take care of and after prolonged arguments, mutual recriminations and endless procrastination *La Finta semplice* was never performed. It was a disappointing setback for Mozart.

As a consolation he had, however, the satisfaction of producing his little Singspiel (German operetta) *Bastien und Bastienne* which he wrote at the suggestion of Dr. Mesmer, the Viennese hypnotist, who had it presented in his own private theatre in October 1768. This one-act German comic opera was made up of simple and graceful arias and duets in *Lied* form, but there

Facsimile of the manuscript of the Andante for piano, K.9b, written by Mozart in Salzburg in 1763 at the age of seven.

Ballroom of the Imperial Palace in Vienna, where Mozart's dances were played.

were already signs of the young composer's confidence in handling his small orchestra (strings, two oboes or flutes and two horns) and an instinct for the theatre. The work faithful to the *Singspiel* form was perhaps the only one of Mozart's compositions to reflect the influence of Gluck.

Thus the days spent in Vienna were by no means time wasted. Apart from his introduction to opera, symphonic music which was then thriving in Vienna further stimulated Wolfgang's interest in the orchestra. The symphonies he produced in Vienna were a major advance on his first essays in this form which he wrote in London a few years earlier. The last compo-

The organ of Salzburg Cathedral.

sitions he wrote in Vienna were a solemn Mass and a march for wind-band. Both were to be played during the consecration of the new church at the orphanage. The ceremony took place on 7 December and Wolfgang conducted in the presence of the Emperor and the court. The Viennese newspapers carried detailed accounts of the occasion emphasizing the young Mozart's central role: "The whole of the music for the festivities has been written anew by Wolfgang Mozart, the twelve-year-old son of Herr Leopold Mozart, *Vice-Kapellmeister* in the service of the Archbishop of Salzburg, whose exceptional talents are renowned. To the general surprise and approval of all those present the composer himself conducted with supreme precision and perfect aplomb and sang the motets as well."

In January 1769 the Mozart family returned to Salzburg.

The visit to Vienna preceded by almost a year the new journey to Italy which was to have great consequences for Wolfgang's musical development. The intervening months were spent in Salzburg in unrelenting studies under his father's strict supervision. A great pleasure awaited Wolfgang on his return to his native city; the Archbishop apparently wishing to salve the trauma of Wolfgang's first defeat in the theatre, had his rejected opera *La Finta semplice* performed in the palace by members of his *Kapelle*. But the *buffo* style was alien to the Archbishop's singers and they failed to do justice to Mozart's first comic opera.

The Archbishop also appointed Wolfgang his Konzertmeister, though without salary.

That year Wolfgang wrote a sizeable quantity of church music. At the same time he also composed instrumental ensembles: divertimenti, cassations and serenades. Such compositions were very popular in Vienna and elsewhere in Southern Austria for that matter and were a favourite both with Leopold Mozart and another Salzburg composer, Michael Haydn, brother of the celebrated Joseph Haydn. Following their lead Wolfgang quickly mastered the style and character of these light musical diversions enriching them with delightful, if unexpected, dramatic and lyrical passages.

Meantime Wolfgang was preparing for a decisive test of his musical prowess. His father was now determined to carry out a long-cherished plan to take his son to Italy, the golden land of music and the one gateway to operatic fame, the country where music flourished and opera thrived.

They left Salzburg in December 1769 carrying a letter of introduction from Hasse, the veteran court composer, then 72.

The Italian adventure eventually resolved itself into three separate visits which affected Mozart's career profoundly. Travelling by way of Innsbruck they first arrived in Rovereto where they had the unexpected pleasure of meeting some of their old friends and people who knew of Wolfgang only from hearsay. After a brief rest at Rovereto Wolfgang played at Baron Todeschi's, and the following day played the organ in the parish church to a huge crowd. In fact, the square before the church was thronged with such an immense sea of humanity that force had to be used to enable Wolfgang to make his way to the organ: several strapping muscular men walked ahead of him clearing the path.

It was the same story in Verona where the Mozarts arrived a few days later. At Verona one of Wolfgang's symphonies was performed and his playing at sight, composing and singing an air to given words caused great astonishment. The effusiveness of Italian music lovers, the big-hearted enthusiastic welcome they accorded him stimulated Wolfgang and amplified the impact of his brilliant performances. The newspapers at Mantua, which the Mozarts visited next, were unanimous in declaring that the boy prodigy from Salzburg had come into the world to eclipse all the recognised masters of music.

Verona, the theater.

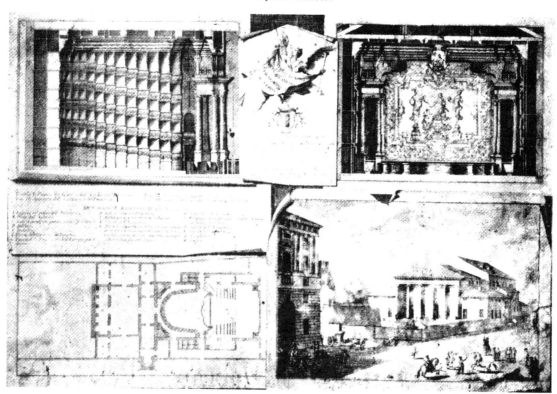

Mozart aged thirteen.
Portrait by Thaddeus
Helbling, 1767 (Oxford
University Press).

The programme of his concerts on the Italian tour showed that Wolfgang had made thorough preparations. It comprised fourteen to fifteen numbers representative of a broad spectrum of musical forms. There were a symphony of his own composition which he conducted at the harpsichord, concertos for harpsichord and violin, which he played solo, and a trio in which Wolfgang took the violin part. The rest of the programme was made up of improvisations of various kinds in a wide range of forms. Wolfgang extemporised on sonatas and fugues, improvised accompaniments to assorted new concertos and arias after just one hearing. He also sang.

Small wonder, therefore, that after the thirteen-year-old genius proved convincingly his complete mastery of even the most complex musical forms that a prestigious opera house in Milan,

Duomo, Florence, in the 18th century.

Rome in the 18th century.

The Sistine Chapel in the 18th century.

View of Naples.

generally regarded as the world's best, commissioned him to write an opera. This commission did not clash with Wolfgang's schedule of further concerts in Italy as he was allowed to take the libretto with him and submit the recitatives in September. He was not expected in Milan until November when, in keeping with tradition, he was to work on the solo parts together with the singers. The opera was to be performed at the next Christmas carnival.

In March 1770 the Mozarts arrived in Bologna, the focal point of musical scholarship in Italy. Leopold Mozart wrote that Wolfgang was more admired in Bologna than anywhere else and anticipated that from Bologna his fame would soon spread all over Italy. And so it did. The most authoritative member of the *Academia Filarmonica* of Bologna at the time was Padre Martini, the celebrated church composer and theorist. Martini's reputation as a teacher was European. A Franciscan monk, he was a man of great mildness, modesty and good nature, always ready to advise and to help. It is difficult to think without emotion of the warm welcome he, the most learned and most revered musician in Europe, gave to Mozart.

Mozart at the age of fourteen. Portrait by C.B. Cignaroli, Verona, January 1770 (Salzburg Mozarteum).

Giovanni Battista Martini, known as Padre Martini (1706-84). Portrait by an unknown artist, about 1775 (Bologna, Liceo Musicale).

During his stay in Bologna Wolfgang studied with Padre Martini carrying away a fugue after each session to work out at home. In every case he acquitted himself to the satisfaction of the outstanding contrapuntist who was positively lost in admiration for the easy grace and style with which the fourteen-year-old boy performed his every assignment.

Leopold Mozart was right in pinning high hopes on Wolfgang's appearance in Bologna as the recommendation of Padre Martini at once gave Wolfgang stature in the eyes of the world.

Further concerts in Florence where the Mozarts stayed almost a month and later in Rome and Naples added to Wolfgang's fame. While there Mozart frequently visited the local opera houses acquainting himself with the manner and performing style of the various singers. The new knowledge helped him in working on his own opera ordered by the Milan opera house.

An idea of Wolfgang's receptiveness, of his phenomenal memory and the extraordinary rapidity with which he absorbed new information can be gauged from the following episode.

Pope Clement XIV with a group of cardinals.

Mozart wearing the Order of the Golden Spur conferred on him by Pope Clement in 1770. Anonymous painting, 1777 (Bologna, Liceo Musicale).

Arriving in Rome in Holy Week the Mozarts went straight to the Sistine Chapel to hear Allegri's *Miserere*, the famous polyphonic work sung annually in the chapel on Good Friday. On that occasion Wolfgang gave convincing proof of his ear and memory by writing down the entire work from memory, after just one hearing.

After Pope Clement XIV conferred on him the Order of the Golden Spur, a distinction which had previously been lavished only on Christoph Gluck, Wolfgang returned to Bologna where he set to work on the opera commissioned by Milan. The two months he had spent in unremitting work under the stimulating supervision of Padre Martini enabled Wolfgang to bring his contrapunctal technique, the most difficult part of musical composition, to a high pitch of perfection. Proof of this came in August 1770 when the *Accademia Filarmonica* of Bologna elected

51

him, a fourteen-year-old boy, a full member after subjecting him to the ordeal of writing for it a contrapunctal setting of a *cantus firmus* (fixed song), although the statutes, besides other qualifications, required that members should be at least twenty.

Revisiting Milan in October Mozart completed the opera ordered by the city's *Teatro Regio Ducale*. *Mitridate Re Di Ponto* (Mithradates, King of Pontus) was produced on 26 December, Wolfgang conducting, with such brilliant success that it was repeated in full houses twenty times (a record for Italy) amid cries of "*Evviva il Maestro! Evviva il Maestrino!*

Mitridate Re Di Ponto was the most accomplished *opera seria* text that Mozart ever set to music, because of the power of Racine's tragedy, on which the librettist Cigna-Santi freely based his own work. Mozart's main concern when starting work on the score was to satisfy the singers; but, since he did not yet

Title page and program of *Mitridate Re di Ponto*.

PRINCEPS  CAETERIQUE
ACADEMICI PHYLHARMONICI.

Omnibus, et singulis praesentes Literas lecturis, felicitatem.

 Uamvis ipsa Virtus sibi, suisque Sectatoribus gloriosum comparet Nomen, attamen pro majori ejusdem majestate publicam in notitiam decuit propagari. Hinc est, quòd hujusce nostrae PHYLHARMONICAE ACADEMIAE existimationi, & incremento consulere, singulorumque Academicorum Scientiam, & profectum patefacere intendentes, Testamur *Dnm Wolfgang. Amadeu Mozart e Salisburg* sub die *Mensis Octobr. Anni* inter Academiae nostrae *Magistros Compositores* adscriptum fuisse. Tanti igitur Coacademici virtutem, & merita perenni benevolentiae monumento prosequentes, hasce Patentes, Literas subscriptas, nostrique Confessus Sigillo impresso obsignatas dedimus.
Bononiae ex nostra Residentia die *Mensis Anni*

Princeps. Petronio Lanzi

a Secretis.

Registr. in Libro Camplono   pag.   *Camploncrius.*

Certificate of Mozart's reception into the Academy of Bologna.

know who they were he began by composing the recitative and then the arias. The latter were, for the most part, stylised but nevertheless possessed considerable dramatic strength and genuine feeling. The opera's brilliant success prompted Count Firmian to commission Mozart to write a further work for the following year—a serenata, *Ascanio in Alba*.

On January 5, 1771, the *Accademia Filarmonica* of Verona not to be outdone by Bologna, bestowed on Wolfgang the title of *Maestro di Cappella*.

Then followed a brief respite from work. Invitations to all kinds of functions and receptions held amid the splendor of the palatial residences of the local nobility followed in quick succession. After a trip to Turin the Mozarts went on to Venice arriving there in time for the famous Carnival and entered into all of its amusements and on the return journey took in Padua. The concerts given by Mozart on the way brought in a handsome

Altar screen and pulpit of St. Mark's, Venice (Anderson photograph).

financial return. He was now firmly established in the favour of the Italian public.

The triumph was complete and father and son, laden with their honours, went back to Salzburg, arriving there on March 28. Orders from Padua for an oratorio and from Milan for another opera were among Wolfgang's trophies, and scarcely had the Mozarts settled down at home before a letter arrived announcing on behalf of the Empress Maria Theresa that Wolfgang would be engaged to write a dramatic serenata for the wedding of Archduke Ferdinand and Princess Maria of Modena to be held in Milan in October.

Accordingly, his stay in Salzburg was to last only a few months. He was back in Italy for the start of the festivities in Milan which opened on October 15, 1772 with the Archduke's entry into the city amid all pomp and circumstance. This was followed by several days of theatrical presentations given in the city's theatre, splendidly bedecked for the occasion. On the first day the opera *Ruggiero*, by the venerable Hasse, was produced along with two glittering ballets which were given in the intermissions. The following day Wolfgang's serenata *Ascanio in Alba* was presented with such success that Leopold felt justified in writing home that his son's serenata had quite eclipsed the opera of their friend and protector. It was repeated the day after and for the rest of the festive season it was given far more frequently than Hasse's opera. But Hasse, with commendable generosity, showed no jealousy. Indeed, he is said to have prophetically remarked: "This boy will throw us all into the shade".

Ascanio in Alba, a *festa teatrale* in two acts, was essentially a pastoral idyll accompanied by ballet scenes. The freshness and exquisite grace of Mozart's melodies, the clarity of form and the composer's delicate flair for harmony, coupled with a free vocal style and the remarkable integrity of the entire work—all this won instant acclaim and general admiration. Besides his fee the Empress Maria Theresa sent Wolfgang a gold watch set with diamonds, with her portrait engraved on the back. This was a token of the highest imperial favour. But the reverse side of the Empress's graciousness was ugly in its haughty and small-minded meanness. Shortly afterwards in a letter to her son, the Archduke Ferdinand, who was toying with the idea of taking the young Mozart into his service, Maria Theresa wrote:

"You ask me about taking into your service the young Salzburg musician. I do not know in what capacity, believing that you have no need for a composer or for useless people. If, however, it would give you pleasure, I do not wish to prevent you. What I say is intended only to urge you not to burden yourself with useless people, and not to give such people permission to

A scene from the private life of Maria Theresa and her family. Drawing by the Archduchess Marie Christine. The little girl with the doll is Marie Antoinette, the boy in the foreground eating cake is Maximilian who later became Archbishop of Cologne and Beethoven's patron (Vienna Österreiche Nationalbibliothek).

Maria Theresa (1717-80) with her family. Her consort Francis I is seated on the left and her eldest son, later Joseph II, is standing on her left. Miniature on paper, 1760, after the painting by Martin van Meytens, about 1752.

represent themselves as belonging in your service. It gives one's service a bad name when such people run about like beggars; he has, besides, a large family."*

The docile Archduke, trained in obedience to his mother naturally thought no more of engaging Mozart, and did not confer any title upon him.

This was, typically, the attitude of aristocratic patrons towards musicians in those days. While exploiting the unique musical talents of the boy prodigy they did not let any thought of being responsible for his welfare and the future of his talent trouble their consciences. They took the view that a court musician's status was not above that of any other of their servants and should not therefore be a burden to them. This attitude perhaps explains why as Wolfgang's unique genius matured and his proud personality took shape, his exalted masters and patrons treated him with frosty indifference. So it was that Wolfgang's brilliant success in Italy proved to be the last "sun beams" of his early glory.

The sixteen-year-old Mozart was on the threshold of a cruel crisis that was to disfigure his future life and career for so long. Neither he nor his father had any inkling of the impending reversal.

The success of the serenata *Ascanio in Alba* enhanced Wolfgang's confidence in his powers and he looked forward to work on his next commission from Milan *Lucio Silla* (Lucius Sulla), an *opera seria* in three acts.

Meantime an uneasy anticipation of an unfavourable change in their fortunes began to worry the Mozarts. During their last absence from Salzburg an event occurred that distressed Wolfgang's father deeply: the old benevolent Archbishop Sigismund von Schrattenbach died and Count Hieronymus Colloredo, a man of despotic inclinations, ill-tempered and tyrannical was named his successor. In fact, Colloredo's election caused universal astonishment and dismay.

Wolfgang was commissioned to compose an opera for the allegiance festival of the new Archbishop. The work chosen was Metastasio's *Il sogno di Scipione'* (The Dream of Scipio), an allegorical *serenata drammatica teatrale* in one act whose appropriateness for the occasion was not evident. But apparently the Archbishop liked it as he offered Wolfgang the position of

---

*12 December 1771, cf. A. Ritter von Arneth, *Briefe der Kaiserin Theresia an ihre Kinder und Freunde*, Vienna, 1881, 1,93.

The Archduchess Marie
Antoinette (1755-93).
Painting by Wagenschoen.

An 18th century map of
the archiepiscopate of
Salzburg (Salzburg
Museum).

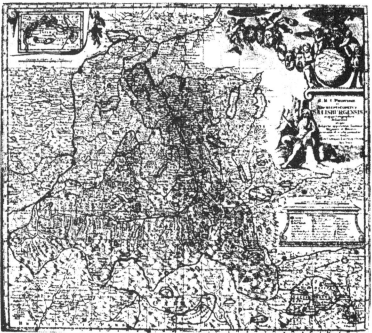

Prince-Archbishop
Sigismund Schrattenbach
(1698-1771). A portrait in
oils.

Membership list of the
Salzburg Court Orchestra,
1775. Leopold Mozart is
listed as the Vice-
Kapellmeister, Wolfgang as
one of the two
Konzertmeisters.

Court *Konzertmeister* with a salary of 150 florins, a decent enough emolument for the time. Wolfgang also received leave of absence to visit Italy in the autumn for the third time.

However, this apparently auspicious start for the Mozarts vis-a-vis their new master soon degenerated into an uneasy troubled relationship. The new Archbishop was irritated by what he saw as Leopold's excessive devotion to the musical interests of his son. He was even more irritated by Wolfgang's independent wit and precocity and especially by his sense of dignity which his extensive travels all over Europe and his fame had stimulated. To the Archbishop all this seemed a breach of propriety on the part of one of his servants. He fully shared Empress Maria Theresa's view that court musicians had no business "to run about like beggars" and that they should put the interests of the *Kapelle* first.

The Archbishop bided his time, however, and even granted the Mozarts leave of absence to enable Wolfgang to go to Milan for the production of his next opera and even agreed to extend their leave of absence. But he also determined that it was high time to bring father and son to heel. Leopold who was shrewd enough to read correctly the radical change in their circumstances under the new Archbishop, decided to concentrate all efforts on securing a suitable position for his son outside Salzburg. Accordingly, he pinned his hopes on the success of Wolfgang's new opera in Milan.

Wolfgang worked on *Lucio Silla* in a feverish burst of musical inspiration and Leopold was happy to see the full power of his son's prodigious gift unfold before his eyes. Indeed, a teenager who had until then enchanted his hearers only with admirable

Manuscript page from the opera *Lucio Silla.*

Archduke Ferdinand of Austria, to whom Mozart dedicated *Lucio Silla.*

LUCIO SILLA

DRAMMA PER MUSICA

DA RAPPRESENTARSI

NEL REGIO-DUCAL TEATRO
DI MILANO

Nel Carnovale dell' anno 1773.

DEDICATO

ALLE LL. AA. RR.

IL SERENISSIMO ARCIDUCA

FERDINANDO

Principe Reale d' Ungheria , e Boemia , Arciduca d' Austria,
Duca di Borgogna , e di Lorena ec. , Cesareo Reale
Luogo-Tenente , Governatore , e Capitano
Generale nella Lombardia Austriaca ,

E LA

SERENISSIMA ARCIDUCHESSA

MARIA RICCIARDA
BEATRICE D'ESTE

PRINCIPESSA DI MODENA.

IN MILANO,

Presso Gio. Batista Bianchi Regio Stampatore
Con licenza de' Superiori.

Title page of *Lucio Silla*.

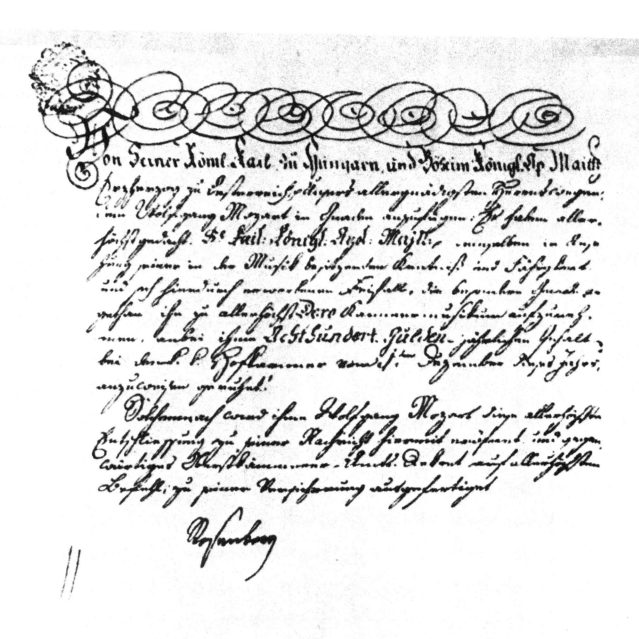

Decree appointing Mozart as Composer of the Imperial Chapel.

Vienna, St. Peter's
Church and Square.
Mozart lived in the house
on the right after leaving
Salzburg in 1781. An
engraving.

imitations of Italian models was now exhibiting unmistakable
signs of a brilliant original individuality.

Unfortunately, Leopold's hopes were dashed as their last trip
to Milan, despite the success of Wolfgang's new opera, failed to
bring about a turn for the better in their fortunes. *Lucio Silla*
was produced on 26 December 1772 at Milan's *Teatro Ducale*
and repeated more than twenty times to crowded and enthusiastic audiences. But for all that and despite the undoubted success of the concerts given by Wolfgang on that occasion Leopold's attempts to secure a permanent position for him at an
Italian court were unsuccessful. Wolfgang received no further
invitation to write for the Italian stage, either. Whenever he ap-
proached Italian patrons about a suitable appointment for his
son, Leopold met with an evasive or non-committal response.
And yet those were the very people who only a short while before were so generous in showering praise on Wolfgang.

A further disappointment awaited Mozart when he arrived in
Vienna. The fickle-hearted Viennese public treated him with
even more indifference than Italy. Leopold wasted two months

A concert in Salzburg
Cathedral. An engraving.

in vain attempts to obtain some court appointment for Wolfgang. No one seemed to be willing enough to take a chance on
the young musician or help him find permanent employment.
Having lost all hope for a betterment of their situation, ex-
hausted and penniless, father and son returned to Salzburg.
Things had come full circle: Wolfgang was again at the mercy
of his despotic master.

Youth

Wolfgang's sustained outburst of creative activity was brought to an abrupt end. By the age of 18 he had been given a taste of the fickleheartedness of the public. He now realized that his artistry as a boy prodigy had been little more than a pleasant diversion and passing attraction for it. Now, at the peak of his powers he found himself chained to a provincial town where everything depressed him: his humiliating dependence on the Prince-Archbishop, the ludicrous haughtiness of the local aristocracy, the stolid narrow-mindedness of the inhabitants and the humdrum routine of provincial life. An English traveler passing through Salzburg described the atmosphere well when he wrote: "The Archbishop prays and hunts, the nobles hunt and pray, the rest of the inhabitants eat, drink and pray".

In Salzburg Mozart was cut off from everything that had given him inspiration in the heady days of his childhood: from concerts, from the theatre and from close association with artistic notables. A musician of world renown found himself reduced to the status of an ordinary menial in the service of a petty tyrant. Every morning Mozart had to sit for hours in the Archbishop's antechamber awaiting, together with the men-servants, His Grace's orders for the day. What is more he had to endure in silence the Archbishop's venomous criticism of his compositions. Colloredo, smugly convinced of the infallibility of his judgement, took it upon himself to correct Mozart's style of composition.

Although Colloredo was energetic, intelligent and well-read he ran his prince-archbishopric with a haughty disdain for the interests of his subjects. His intolerance and domineering manner made it difficult even for his equals to bear with him. He absolutely insisted on the total obedience of his subordinates. To those who meekly accepted the need for complete submission he was sometimes kind, in his own small way. But he was merciless to those who displayed even a shadow of independence. It was hardly surprising, therefore, that his attitude to the Mozarts, which initially was cautious, gradually degenerated into open hostility. He saw to it that Leopold was kept out of the mainstream of musical life at court but refrained from dismissing him altogether. From the first days of Wolfgang's service as *Konzertmeister* until the final rupture, the Archbishop never gave up his attempts to break the proud youth, to browbeat him into submission. And, rather paradoxically, he was doing this to a young man whose fame and unique musical talent could not but flatter his self-esteem.

The Archbishop worked steadily towards his goal his chief

weapons being rudeness and the various indignities he heaped on Wolfgang and his father. One example was the petty tutelage he established over Wolfgang's conduct, his relations with other people, and even his creative work. An extremely vain and supercilious man, Colloredo saw his own taste as the chief criterion in judging the merits of Mozart's works. Actually, however, his taste was limited and very conservative. He was a zealous devotee of the old Italian school both in the field of church music and in instrumental music. He did not permit the inclusion of any local folk-song elements in music, allowing them, with great reluctance, only in divertimenti, cassations and similar forms of light musical entertainment which accompanied his elaborate feasts. The Archbishop had nothing but contempt for theatrical music.

Quite possibly, such an abrupt reversal of his fortunes would have broken a lesser artist or a man lacking the courage of his convictions. Not so with Mozart. His dynamic resilient personality coupled with his sense of humour and cheerfulness enabled him to endure all trials and eventually win through.

The judgement of history upon Archbishop Colloredo is that he did not recognize, or did not wish to have it recognized, that he had a genius in his service. This constitutes not a sin, however, but simply a lack of insight or of goodwill. Then again the whole atmosphere of provincial Salzburg was against Mozart. Salzburg was too small a place for a genius of Mozart's calibre

Mozart playing his music for the Viennese aristocracy.

who wished, among other things, to write operas and not just the church music that the Archbishop expected of him. Operas he could write only for other places—Munich, Vienna, Milan, or Venice. What Colloredo needed was not a genius, always wanting to go on leave, but a modest conscientious musician for his *Kapelle*, faithful to his duties. Thus, on his side, cold unfriendliness gained the upper hand, and on Wolfgang's side a feeling of injury and of hatred, which steadily grew because the Archbishop determined that it had to be suppressed.

Mozart found his comfort and consolation in the friendly atmosphere of his family, and in the informality of the company of his friends, but primarily in his creative work. When absorbed in composing he felt neither his loneliness nor his humiliation at the hands of Colloredo. He was in his element then and could spread his wings.

The rich fund of musical knowledge and impressions he had stored up during his brilliantly successful concert tours that took him through almost every European capital was now taking on a new significance. As a child, he had absorbed the peculiarities of the musical speech of various nations with the ease of all children learning to speak foreign languages. He mastered and incorporated into his own musical idiom the smooth and graphic style of Italian vocalism, and the easy grace and free-flowing rhythm of French melodies. There is little doubt that as the melodic thinking of the child Mozart developed, he was influenced by the intimate sincerity and intonations of the various Bohemian Slovak and Hungarian songs which he had heard both in their natural state in Salzburg and as transformed in the music of Viennese composers.

During his cloistered days in Salzburg Mozart worked relentlessly to perfect his musical philosophy. In the crucible of his unique genius elements drown from the music of other peoples that he had accepted as akin to his own, were transformed and fused into an integrated if, at times, contradictory, melodic wealth.

At this stage Wolfgang was mastering not just the external features of folk and professional music, he was penetrating its very soul—its message, and character. As a result familiar and standard patterns of melody which Wolfgang used as extensively as did other composers of the day, in his interpretation, became ennobled often in unexpected ways, were full of inspired spirituality, and freshness. Mozart was possessed of what is perhaps the greatest quality of a man of genius—to see and hear everything anew.

Mozart was engaged in a reassessment of the creative trends in European music he had discovered during his extensive con-

Johann Christian Bach (1735-82). One of two portraits by Thomas Gainsborough.

cert tours of Europe. While valuing the compositions of his father and those of his closest friends whose techniques he continued to develop, Wolfgang's own preferences increasingly inclined him towards new progressive elements which were in accord with his own ideas on the musical embodiment of the spirit of the times.

He gravitated towards the exalted dramatic spirit of Italian opera, towards the caressing and impetuous sonority of Christian Bach's sonatas, and the passionate upward flights of Schobert. Bearing in mind Mozart's consummate composing skill, which was always his hallmark, it becomes clear that the period of maturing which usually sees productive, if still ill-defined, tentative gropings, in the case of Mozart was quite different.

The compositions he produced as a youth are remarkable both for their technical brilliance, the wide range of music forms they cover, and for the rich diversity of the ideas, feelings and moods they capture. Thus among his vast output of humorous, light-hearted, festive or solemn symphonies symphony in

Mozart by John Zoffany, about 1765.

G minor stands out as a harbinger of the future mournful and passion-filled images of the mature Mozart. Also unusual for this period was his harpsichord sonata in G major which is at once dynamic and contemplative, and his famous Minuet in D major, which is part of a divertimento noted for its sublime poetry.

The years of Mozart's youth also saw the emergence of his highly individual harpsichord style with its sincere singing quality and flexibility. Its vivacious and ingenuous intonations made Mozart's music for harpsichord sound so much like lively conversation.

Mozart's violin concertos written in that period were even more striking in terms of completeness and integrity. As a performer Mozart did not devote nearly as much time to the violin as he did to the harpsichord. And yet he played the violin with an inspired virtuosity that was beyond most of the foremost violinists of the day. He had his own view on violin playing technique as is evidenced by the following comment he made on the performing style of Lolli, a leading Italian violinist who, like him, had entered the service of the Archbishop of Salzburg: "I am not in favour of terrific tempos for the sake of which only half of the instrument's potential is used and one has to play almost 'in the air', as it were, barely touching the strings with the bow." Mozart did not believe in virtuosity for virtuosity's sake, whether in singing, in harpsichord or violin playing. He recognised only one type of virtuosity, that which enabled the performer to convey the impulsiveness of human emotions, the rapidity of thought or carefree gaiety. This kind of virtuosity was integral to the expressive arsenal of Mozart's musical language.

This blend of virtuosity, perfect form and heartfelt lofty poetry permeates every melodic phrase and cadence and places Mozart's violin concertos among the supreme achievements in this branch of music. Mozart wrote violin concertos in profusion skilfully combining challenging artistic tasks with an easy accessibility and graphic expressiveness of melodic material. He wrote them with an eye to a wide democratic audience as if ignoring the judgement of his haughty but undiscerning master and submitting them, instead, to the verdict of posterity.

In Salzburg Mozart lived in comfortable enough circumstances. The family moved from their rather cramped dwelling on the bank of the Salzach river, where Wolfgang was born, into more spacious and comfortable quarters which Leopold furnished with loving care and impeccable taste to create congenial surroundings for his son. Nannerl and Wolfgang were friends with the children of the solid middle-class Salzburg families. Before long, however, Wolfgang's outstanding talents opened to him the doors of many aristocratic homes where he gave music lessons and played at private concerts. Wolfgang's quick and lively wit, his good breeding and inborn sense of social graces, his dignity, everything that so infuriated the Archbishop usually attracted to him members of the local elite. Apart from church music for the Archbishop Mozart also wrote pieces for these families which were performed at private concerts. Even these compositions written routinely to order were easily superior to the mediocre generality of music for domestic entertainment.

While encouraging Wolfgang's association with the city's leading families Leopold was at the same time careful not to de-

Leopold Mozart.
Anonymous portrait,
about 1765 (Salzburg
Mozarteum).

ter him from his youthful inclination towards simple diversions. Leopold had withdrawn from the mainstream of social life and confined himself to the narrow circle of his family friends and fellow musicians. He devoted most of his time to his duties as organist in the local Cathedral. A devout Christian, Leopold sought to encourage his son's interest in church music and zealously rehearsed with the choir Wolfgang's choral compositions.

Sacred music was the Archbishop's particular concern and Wolfgang had to write a good deal of it. He enjoyed writing for the choir as he was greatly excited by the harmony of human voices singing in perfect unison. The imagery associated with the subjects of Mozart's music for the church often took on a vivid dramatic dimension. And yet his nostalgia for opera, for dramatic music, continued. Neither the tender care which was lavished on him in the family nor the fleeting infatuations he experienced in that period could dull, still less suppress, the steadily increasing sense of dissatisfaction that he often felt. Not after that stimulating and incomparable feeling of creative uplift which enveloped him when he worked with feverish enthusiasm on his first operas for the Italian stage.

Ironically, now that his dramatic gift was in full flower, Mozart found himself cut off from the theatre. And he could hardly entertain any hope of writing another opera soon. The Archbishop did not approve of the musical theatre. Nor was opera in particular favour in Germany. True, towards the end of his second year in the Archbishop's service Fortune smiled on

The conference room of the Archbishop's *Residenz* or palace, Salzburg. Many of Mozart's chamber works were written for performance here.

him again when suddenly he received an operatic commission from Munich.

On December 6 the father and son started for Munich, where Wolfgang was engaged through the influence of one of his patrons to compose an opera for the Carnival of 1775. The idea had been suggested to the Bavarian Elector by Count Ferdinand von Zeil. The Archbishop of Salzburg could not refuse so influential a client. Shortly afterwards Wolfgang received the libretto of an *opera buffa, La Finta giardiniera* (The Pretended Gardener Maid). The rather banal plot was based on a string of confusing misunderstandings that beset two pairs of lovers. The libretto by Ranieri de' Calzabigi (Gluck's literary collaborator) had to be revamped in rather a hurry. But Mozart was not put off by flaws in the libretto. Stimulated, no doubt, by the rich resources at his command, Wolfgang exerted himself to the utmost. The text of *La Finta giardiniera* had already been set to music earlier by Pasquale Anfossi, and the score was familiar to Mozart who used it as a framework to his own composition. A novel feature of the work was the clear division into serious and comic parts. Mozart himself wrote a series of arias, some of them very beautiful. But because the characters were not too well-defined, nor sufficiently distinctive, some of the concerted numbers were not as effective as they might have been. For all that the opera made for pleasant listening and was yet another example of Mozart's creative genius. Produced on 13 January at Munich's Hoftheater the opera was a great success. Schubert, a leading music critic of the day commented in *Deutsche Chronik* on Mozart's "wonderful genius" and added: "Unless Mozart should prove to be a mere overgrown product of the greenhouse, he will be the greatest composer that ever lived."

After the triumph in Munich the thought of having to return to Salzburg and back to the hateful drudgery of his routine duties as the Archbishop's *Konzertmeister* was intolerable. More hateful still was the prospect of becoming the target of further indignities heaped on him by his tyrannical master who insisted on Wolfgang's placing himself totally at the mercy of his wishes and strict dull routine. Nor was Wolfgang particularly heartened by his new commission from the Archbishop, a serenata in two acts, *"Il Re Pastore"* (The Shepherd King) which had to be composed in great haste for a visit to Salzburg by the Archduke Maximilian. Given a basically static text of the libretto Mozart supplied a score which was largely instrumental. The style of the opera proved to be much more robust and concise than that of Mozart's Milanese operas, from *Mitridate* to *Lucio Silla*, revealing the composer as a musical personality of note.

Although the opera was performed at the Archbishop's palace

Title page of the German version of *La Finta Giardiniera*.

Manuscript page from the opera *La Finta Giardiniera*.

Munich. An engraving. In the center is the Frauenkirche and to the right is the Elector's Palace where Wolfgang and Nannerl appeared with such success.

Romerberg Square in Frankfurt.

Joseph Haydn (1732-1809). Portrait in oils by Thomas Hardy, 1791 (London, Royal College of Music).

with considerable success, Mozart did not entertain any illusions for its future. This mood of disillusionment comes through in his letters to his old friend and former teacher Padre Martini.

. . . "Most beloved and esteemed Signore, Padre Maestro! I beg you most earnestly to tell me, frankly and without reserve what you think of my latest compositions. We live in this world in order to learn zealously and, by interchanging our ideas, to enlighten one another, and thus endeavour to promote science and art. Oh, how often have I longed to be near you, most Reverend Father, so that I might be able to talk to and reason with you. I live in a country where music leads a struggling existence, though indeed, apart from those who have left us, we still have excellent teachers and particularly composers of wisdom, learning and taste. As for the theatre, we are in a bad way for lack of singers. We have no *castrati*, and we shall never have them as they insist on being handsomely paid; and generosity is not one of our faults. Meanwhile I am amusing myself by writing chamber music and music for the church, in which branches of composition we have two other excellent masters of counterpoint, Signori Haydn and Adlgasser. My father is in the service of the Cathedral and this gives me an opportunity of writing as much church music as I like . . . Alas, we are so far apart, my very dear Signore Padre Maestro! If we were together, I should have so many things to tell you! . . . I long to win your favour and I never cease to grieve that I am far away from that one person in the world whom I love, revere and esteem most of all . . ." The letter shows the full measure of Wolfgang's creative loneliness and his fervent dream of breaking out of the straightjacket of Salzburg and the Archbishop's service.

But this letter, too, was without result. And it was impossible to leave against the will of the Archbishop. Meanwhile the tension between master and servant became unbearable. Wolfgang realised full well that he was a kind of hostage. He feared that the moment he broke with the Archbishop the latter would immediately dismiss his father. Where would that leave the family? What would be the consequences for his mother and sister?

Salzburg. An engraving by Mozart's contemporary, Franz von Neumann.

And so he had to endure patiently further abuse and indignities from the Archbishop, although each sharp comment to the quick-tempered and proud youth was like the lash of a whip.

And yet, at long last, Mozart succeeded in realising his dream, but at a price. In March 1777, Leopold, pleading the "unhappy circumstances" of his family asked for a leave of absence to go on tour, but to this request Colloredo seems to have given not even an unfavourable answer—simply none at all. He forestalled a further attempt on Leopold's part by requiring his *Kapelle* to be in full readiness for a visit of the Emperor Joseph II, who was to pass through Salzburg. When after the visit, Leopold tried once more, he received a flat refusal with the remark that Wolfgang, as "only a half-time servant anyway, could be permitted to travel alone". But when Wolfgang wanted to follow the suggestion, the Archbishop raised new objections. What was left but revolt? On 1 August 1777 Wolfgang asked for his dismissal, formulating his reasons in a letter to the Archbishop as follows:

". . . Most Gracious Prince and Lord! Parents endeavour to place their children in a position to earn their own bread . . . The greater the talents which children have received from God, the more are they bound to use them for the improvement of their own and their parents' circumstances . . . The Gospel teaches us to use our talents in this way. My conscience tells me that I owe it to God to be grateful to my father, who has spent his time unswearingly upon my education, so that I may lighten his burden, look after myself and later on be able to support my sister . . ."

Eight days later the Archbishop wrote the dry and biting comment on Wolfgang's letter:

"Referred to the Chancellery with the decision that father and son, in accordance with the Gospel, have permission to seek their fortune elsewhere".* Later the Archbishop relented somewhat and cancelled the dismissal of Leopold and inflicted no further humiliation on him.

Wolfgang was free to go and seek his fortune in other cities. But this time the thought of going to Italy or even to Vienna was far from his mind: the recent failures he had suffered in both places still rankled with him. He planned on entering the service of a German prince in either Munich or Mannheim or at least on making some money by giving public recitals there and then push on to Paris where he hoped to find both fame and employment.

---

*A. Einstein, Mozart, p. 47, Cassella Co. Ltd, 1947.

Christian Cannabich, conductor
of the Mannheim orchestra.

The Mannheim theater.

Augsburg, Leopold
Mozart's native city,
about 1760.

On 23 September, 1777 Mozart, in fine spirits, set out with
his mother, who was to take his father's place in advising him
as Wolfgang lacked common sense, the necessary business acu-
men and was too trusting. It was a wrench for Leopold to part
with his wife and son. From the experience of earlier travels he
knew the sort of difficulties and problems that lay ahead for
Wolfgang on the new concert tour as he would be denied the
benefit of his father's guidance.

His son, however, breathed freely; the deliverance from a position he had long groaned under was delightful enough to miti-
gate even the pain of separation from his father and sister. Fortunately for him he could not foresee the life which lay before
him—a life full of trials and disappointments, and with so few
joys.

Wolfgang wrote frequent letters to his father in which he described everything he met on the way emphasising, naturally,
the musical milieu of the cities he passed through. Leopold
closely scrutinised these letters for signs of a favourable change
in his son's affairs. Unfortunately, Wolfgang was in for a series
of disappointments at the very start of the tour.

His first stopping place was Munich where his opera *La Finta
giardinera* had enjoyed such great success two years previously
(1777), but was not successful in his efforts to obtain a permanent appointment. It appeared that none of the local grandees
had a vacancy for Mozart.

None of his former patrons could or would help him now, although they were all delighted to hear his music at their private concerts.

From Munich they went to Mannheim by way of Augsburg, Leopold's home town. Their visit to Augsburg, however, was without profitable results and they reached Mannheim on October 30. The city was one of the centers of musical life in Germany and had a reputable symphony orchestra which was formed in the 1740s by Johann Stamitz, a celebrated composer and conductor. Mannheim also had an excellent opera house, the principal lure for Mozart.

In the camaraderie-dominated community of the local music-makers Wolfgang was in his element. He made many friendships in Mannheim which later stimulated his creative genius. Although the good prospects which seemed to open before him initially were not realised, the visit marked a decisive stage in Mozart's life. In Mannheim he wrote two wonderful concertos for flute and oboe intended for August Wendling, the outstanding virtuoso flutist from the Mannheim symphony orchestra, and oboist Friedrich Ramm, respectively. Mozart also produced a number of violin sonatas which reflected his impressions of the Mannheim orchestra: they were noted for a lofty style, love of contrast and a slow building-up of sound which was so much a feature of the style of Mannheim symphonists.

Mozart's theatrical impressions were not vivid. In Mannheim Mozart met Ignaz Holzbauer, a noted German composer for the theatre, and heard his Singspiel *"Gunther von Schwarzburg"*. Having been until then chiefly attracted by Italian opera Mozart suddenly saw the urgency of the problem of creating a national German operatic theatre.

Also in Mannheim he had the good fortune of meeting the well-known German poet Wieland, an encounter that was to have important consequences. When working on *Die Zauberflote (The Magic Flute)* Mozart drew heavily on a fairy-tale, *"Lulu Oder die Zauberflote"* from Wieland's *Dschinnistan*. The irreligious and free-wheeling atmosphere in which Mannheim sought to rival Paris appealed to Mozart very much.

But everything Mozart experienced and discovered on the professional side in Mannheim was overshadowed by a purely personal experience that flared up suddenly. During his sojourn in Mannheim he fell in love with a violence that robbed him of the ability to judge his position objectively. Until then his life had been entirely devoted to music and fleeting youthful infatuations befell him but rarely. Mozart liked to think of himself as being more mind than heart and often poked fun at the suitors of his sister. But his encounter with Aloysia Weber positively swept him off his feet.

Aloysia was the second daughter of Fridolin Weber, prompter and copyist. She was a gifted singer, with a fine voice and considerable beauty. She made a due impression upon Wolfgang who wrote to Leopold, "Her father is an honest man and a strict teacher of his children. For fifteen years he has had to content himself with a salary of 420 francs and on this puny sum had to support his wife and six children. His fifteen-year-old daughter sings most admirably and has a lovely pure voice. She somewhat lacks the dramatic ability needed to become the prima donna of any reputable theatre."

Aloysia returned Wolfgang's attachment and allowed him to teach her singing. At the end of January 1778 as he was growing increasingly fond of Aloysia Mozart created a delightful Italian aria for her which she performed wonderfully.

Wolfgang wrote in a letter of February 28, 1778 to his father: "For practice I have also set to music the aria *Non so d'onde viene*, etc. which has been so beautifully composed by Bach . . . At first I had intended it for Raaff, but the beginning

Mannheim, the Elector's Palace. A drawing (Schenk, *Mozart and His Times).*

seemed to me too high for his voice. Yet I liked it so much that I would not alter it; and from the orchestral accompaniment, too, it seemed to me better suited to a soprano. So I decided to write it for Mlle Weber. Well, I put it aside and started off on the words *Se al labbro* for Raaff. But all in vain! I simply could not compose as the first aria kept on running in my head. So I returned to it and made up my mind to compose it exactly for Mlle Weber's voice . . . This is now the best aria she has and she will win success wherever she sings it."

Love introduced a new dash of colour into Mozart's life and art: impulsive dreaminess and a profound dramatic feeling.

He lingered on in Mannheim without taking any practical steps, losing all track of time and delaying the decision to move on. At one point, touched by the Weber family's poverty he even conceived the plan of taking Aloysia to Italy and there writing a new opera for her first appearance. His mother was unable to dissuade him. It took an angry letter from his father to rescue Wolfgang from the vicious circle. It is understandable that Leopold, at the thought of his son's wandering through the world in the role of musical gypsy and composing factotum for a budding prima donna almost went out of his mind. Urging upon Wolfgang the doubtful character of his plan Leopold used all the powers of persuasion to tear him away from the dangerous surroundings:

"Off with you to Paris, and that soon! Find your place among those who are really great—*aut Caesar, aut nihil!* The mere thought of seeing Paris ought to have preserved you from all these flighty ideas. From Paris the name and fame of a man of talent resound throughout the world". . .

Leopold was convinced that Paris was the only city where Wolfgang stood any chance of securing a suitable position or obtaining a lucrative commission. It was a hard struggle for Wolfgang, but his love for his father made him defer to his authority and the date for departure was fixed.

Before leaving, however, he gave some public recitals and produced a number of compositions of admirable quality. And now for the first time Mannheim became aware of what it was losing. Parting with the Webers was a wrench for Mozart: they all wept and thanked him as their "greatest benefactor". Leaving Mannheim on 14 March, 1778 he reached Paris on the 23.

Unfortunately Leopold's anticipations did not on this occasion prove correct. As always Paris was busily pursuing its social whirl. But Wolfgang remained outside its mainstream. His efforts to obtain commissions or engagements to give public or private concerts were largely unsuccessful.

Disappointed and embittered, Mozart rushed about the city

trying to reestablish old contacts and look up his father's Parisian friends. But few in Paris retained any recollections of those exciting days when the *creme de la creme* of the city's aristocracy flocked to those brilliant concerts by the astonishing wonder-child from Salzburg.

Their old friend Grimm was still there but by no means so devoted to their interests as he had been. Wolfgang at 22 was not the same attraction as the boy prodigy had been and the musical world of Paris was totally absorbed in the Gluck and Piccinni war. At the time of Mozart's arrival the strife between the Piccinnists and the Gluckists was at its height and so Mozart was "allowed" to spend his days in Paris quietly and unobserved.

Only a few of the father's remaining friends in Paris showed any interest in Wolfgang and were able to organise for him poorly paid music lessons for some high-society families. In this way he made the acquaintance of the Duc de Guines who played the flute and his daughter who played the harp. Mozart was surprised at the quite decent technique of both, but the father's ambitions went further as he wanted his daughter to compose as well.

In the composition lessons he gave the daughter, for which payment was always late, Mozart suffered all the torments of the impatient teacher (letter of 14 May):

View of Mannheim.

"It is extremely doubtful whether she has any talent for composition, especially as regards invention and ideas. Well, we shall see. If she gets no inspiration or ideas (for at present she really has none whatever), then it is to no purpose, for—God knows—I can't give her any".

For several months Mozart unsuccessfully tried to kindle a creative spark in her then, fortunately for both teacher and pupil, she steamed into the calmer waters of a happy marriage, so that when Mozart came for the next lesson a maid thrust his fee into his hand, unfortunately only half of what was due! The only tangible result of this acquaintance was a concerto for harp

Title page for an early English edition of Mozart's A major Violin Sonata, K.305, written in Mannheim in 1778 (Ates Orga).

and flute written by Mozart at the request of the Duke, for which work the former was never paid.

The four months he spent in Paris gave him few joys. True, a symphony he wrote there was warmly received at a public concert. But he was not given the opportunity of writing an opera as he had hoped. Noverre, the famous theorist of the ballet, promised to use his influence in Mozart's favour. But all he did was to engage him to compose twelve pieces for his ballet *Les petits riens*, again for nothing. What is more the ballet was produced six times but neither the announcement nor the newspapers ever mentioned Mozart's name.

But the worst was yet to come: in the dog days of June 1778 his mother became seriously ill and died in his arms on July 3. It was a dark hour when, on 4 July he had to beg the old family friend in Salzburg, Abbe Bullinger to prepare his father for the news of the death of his wife. In a long and rambling letter to his father he tried to conceal the sad truth but to Bullinger he opened his heart: "Mourn with me, my friend. This has been the saddest day of my life—I am writing this at two in the morning. I have to tell you that my mother my dear mother, is no more. She died without regaining consciousness, her life blown out like a candle."

The following day Wolfgang buried her. Grief-stricken as he was, he knew he had to soldier on. And so he did. After the funeral he went back, with remarkable quickness, to his own affairs. From the hotel he soon moved to Melchior Grimm's quarters. But the reproaches Grimm levelled against Wolfgang for his lack of practical sense and failure to win the interest of important people only served to irritate him. Mozart gradually realised that his trip to Paris would produce no results and open up no prospect, yet the thought of having to return to Salzburg was most galling to him.

His father's letters became more frequent. Crushed by the death of his wife, he was further dismayed by his son's failures in Paris and was afraid lest Wolfgang should take some ill-considered decision on the spur of the moment; for himself he was willing to accept his fate and expected no miracles to happen. When the Archbishop offered him the position of Court Composer which fell vacant and to Wolfgang the post of *Konzertmeister* Leopold began to urge his son to take up the offer. Wolfgang played for time although his procrastination began to irritate Leopold.

During the last months of freedom he had in Paris Wolfgang completed a number of harpsichord sonatas whose maturity and dramatic quality were far superior to anything he had written for the harpsichord before.

Mozart's mother, Anna-Maria. Portrait by an unknown artist, about 1775 (Salzburg Mozarteum).

In September 1778, surrendering to his father's pressure, Mozart decided very reluctantly to return to Salzburg. But he made the conditions that he should no longer be burdened with the duty of playing the violin in the Archbishop's service, and that he should conduct and accompany arias at the keyboard, for he wished to be sure of the succession to the post of *Kapellmeister*.

Meantime the father urged him to expedite his return to Salzburg fearing as much the Archbishop's ire as a possible change of heart by his son. Wolfgang was indeed delaying his return and with good cause. On the way he unexpectedly made a detour to Mannheim to visit the Webers. Early in September, however, the Webers had left Mannheim and followed the court

Mozart's letter to the
Abbé Bullinger about the
death of his mother, 3
July 1778. Facsimile of
the last page (Salzburg
Mozarteum).

The Mozart family. From a painting by Johann Nepomuk de la Croce, 1780-81. The mother's
portrait hangs on the wall (Salzburg Mozarteum).

Manuscript of the F minor harpsichord sonata, which Mozart wrote a few days after his mother died.

to Munich where Aloysia was now engaged as a leading soprano at the local opera house. Mozart went to Munich hoping to see her. But he was in for a shock: a beautiful and talented opera singer, Aloysia was enjoying great success and had thus lost whatever interest she might have felt in the young Mozart, and there was certainly no further need for his protection.

In the middle of January 1779, in mourning for his mother, disappointed in his first love, and with all his hopes dashed, Wolfgang Amadeus Mozart returned to Salzburg, the home of his childhood. The Archbishop had won again.

Idomeneo

Two uneventful years in the stifling provincial atmosphere of Salzburg went by, another two years of humiliation for Mozart. The Archbishop compelled him to agree to crippling conditions: he was not to give public recitals or absent himself from Salzburg for however brief a period without permission.

In the meantime Colloredo's attitude became more callous and insensitive, and the indignities he heaped on Mozart more humiliating. A relationship which had been strained at the best of times was rapidly degenerating into mutual hatred.

To make matters worse, Wolfgang could no longer look to his father for total moral support. Leopold was growing old and weak and was withdrawing into religion. He had despaired of effecting a favourable change in his son's fortunes and was now urging him to submission. Nannerl, Wolfgang's sister, who took over the running of the household after their mother's death sided with the father. Thus Wolfgang found himself in increasing isolation even in his own family.

As Mozart matured his dream of writing for the theatre was becoming more intense. This urge to write opera continued throughout his life, in fact—big opera with a large orchestra. He needed opera on the grand scale. And Italy had taught him that opera constituted the highest ecstasy of art: all the forms and devices of music culminating in the most beautiful of instruments, the human voice, and dramatic passion transfigured in a magic medium of expression.

In order to compose operas Mozart was prepared to make every sacrifice; he even overcame his dislike of the French language, French singers, and the French public. He would compose in every form: *opera seria* or *opera buffa*, Singspiel or "machine"-opera in either German or Italian. His attempts to write music for wandering theatrical troupes who visited Salzburg from time to time were doomed to failure, however, as they lacked the necessary funds. That was the reason why he

IDOMENEO.

DRAMMA

PER

MUSICA

DA RAPPRESENTARSI
NEL TEATRO NUOVO DI

CORTE

PER COMANDO
DI S. A. S E.

CARLO TEODORO

Conte Palatino del Rheno, Duca dell'
alta, e baſſa Baviera, e del Palatinato
Superiore, etc. etc. Archidapifero,
et Elettore, etc. etc.

NEL CARNOVALE
1781.

La Poesia è del Signor Abate Giambattista Varesco
Capellano di Corte di S. A. R. l'Arcivescovo, e Principe di Salisburgo.
La Musica è del Signor Maestro Wolfgango Ama-
deo Mozart Academico di Bologna, e di Verona, in
in attual servizio di S. A. R. l'Arcivescovo, e Principe
di Salisburgo.
La Traduzione è del Signor Andrea Schachtner,
pure in attual servizio di S. A. R. l'Arcivescovo, e
Principe di Salisburgo.

MONACO,
Apreſſo Francesco Giuseppe Thuille.

Title page of *Idomeneo*.

Model of stage set from the original Munich production of *Idomeneo*.

left unfinished the music he wrote for Gebler's *Thames, König in Aegypten (Thomas, King of Egypt)* at the suggestion of the impresario Bohm, and separate numbers for *"Zaide"*, a Singspiel (German operetta), which had been intended for Bohm's successor, Emanuel Schikaneder (the future librettist of *The Magic Flute*).

Rescue from the hateful drudgery of the Archbishop's service came when Mozart least expected it. At the end of 1780 a real chance offered itself. Through the efforts of his friends at Munich he received a commission to write a grand *opera seria* for the Carnival of 1781, and a most congenial employment it proved to be. As a result of it Mozart composed his *Idomeneo Re di Creta (Idomeneo, King of Crete)*, a work unique among his creations. As the Archbishop of Salzburg was careful to keep his relations with the Electoral Court of Munich on an even keel he could not very well refuse the Elector and, with great reluctance, granted his rebellious *Konzertmeister* leave of absence for a trip to Munich.

At last Mozart had all the required means at his disposal: the combined orchestras of Mannheim and Munich, excellent singers, and a highly discriminating court as an audience.

The subject of *Idomeneo Re di Creta* was based on the classical Greek legend of Troy. The libretto given to Mozart by Abbate Varesco, court chaplain at Salzburg, was overburdened with detail and the characters were rather ill-defined and larger than life. For all the flaws of the libretto which Varesco had adapted from the French original in rather a hurry Mozart set to work in a burst of musical inspiration. This was his first opportunity to exert his full powers as a composer. It was his chance to shine and he was not going to miss it.

At the very first rehearsals Mozart's music for *Idomeneo* with its many innovations, was highly approved by the Elector and his court. Leopold even wrote to him from Salzburg: "The universal subject of conversation here is your opera." The first performance of *Idomeneo* took place at Munich's Hoftheater on January 29, 1781. It was a huge success and decided once and for all Mozart's position as a dramatic composer.

For the first time there was clear evidence of the complete awakening of Mozart's dramatic instinct: a conflict between the composer and the librettist.

The material Varesco had to handle was not bad and it was familiar to everyone in its Biblical version. But it was not particularly good material for an opera. However Mozart, with the experiences of Mannheim and Paris behind him, would not have set it to music if he had found it completely unsuitable. Varesco had his product printed in unabridged form. But Mozart altered it with complete freedom. Brevity was always his motto. He never dreamed of setting to music all the stanzas Varesco had provided for the chorus numbers. His careful attention extended to the smallest detail, such as the placing of resonant vowels, as well as to the most important matters, such as scenic convenience and the total scenic effect. As a result, the combination of two basic components of opera—the psychological as expressed by Electra's rage and the people's despair, and the scenic (the storm) recalled dramatic scenes from Gluck but had a far greater emotional power and scenic effect.

Idomeneo was, in operatic form, a drama of unprecedented freedom and daring. It was an *opera seria* unlike any other. At Munich for the premiere of his opera, Mozart met many of his old musical friends of his Mannheim days all of whom were delighted with the opera. The Elector himself expressed his admiration and also surprise that, as he put it, "such great things are tucked away in so small a head".

Mozart embarked on his career as an operatic composer at a time when the musical theatre was on the threshold of a radical and far-reaching change. The Italian *opera seria* (serious opera) whose undivided rule on the European stage was until then unchallenged entered a deep crisis: the conflict between the dramatic and the musical components of *opera seria* which had emerged early in the 18th century resulted in *opera seria* becoming more like a concert theatrical presentation in full dress. A typical opera seria would be a brilliant suite made up of virtuoso arias and duets linked together by the recitative. But in most cases it was an elaborate court presentation devoid of any true dramatic content and soon became the object of ridicule on the part of the forward-looking supporters of new ideas.

The emergence of comic opera (*opera-buffa*) dealt a body blow to *opera seria*. *Opera buffa*, the product of the infinite ingenuity and irrepressible sense of humour of the Italian people made its first conquest of the theatre in the 1730s. The chief strengths of *opera buffa* were a realistic plot and life-size characters. It also had a certain amount of bite as light-hearted commentary on the contemporary social scene. The roots of comic opera can be found in *La Serva Padrona* (The Maid Mistress), by Giovanni Pergolesi. When it was produced in Paris by the Bambini company in 1752 it immediately became the subject of heated controversy, giving rise to the famous *"Guerre des Bouffons"* as the acrimonious polemic about Italian opera came to be known. The war divided musicians and music lovers into two camps, those in favour of French music (as represented by Lulli and Rameau) and those carrying the flag for Italian opera. Although

Christoph Willibald
Gluck (1714-87).
Engraving by Auguste de
Saint-Aubin, 1781.

initially the former seemed to have gained the upper hand and
the king of France ordered the Italian troupe out of the country
the eventual victory was with the Italians. A few years later national comic opera companies were established in England, in
Germany and in France.

At the height of the universal enthusiasm for *opera buffa* it
seemed that it would oust *opera seria* completely. But the latter
proved to have deep roots and would not surrender without a
fight. The remarkable integrity of its arioso style, the enchanting beauty of its vocalism and exalted sentiments expressed (the
latter stemmed from its association with classical mythology)
continued to appeal to outstanding musicians and music lovers
alike. As the dramatic weakness of *opera seria* became more apparent composers wishing to work in this noble form were increasingly aware of the need to strike out in new directions.

Attempts to reform heroic operas had been made before. But the efforts of composers in different countries, some of whom produced, on occasion, considerable results, paled into insignificance beside what the great Viennese composer Christoph Gluck did. Gluck's noble genius and innovations conferred on *opera seria* an extraordinary sense of sublime simplicity. The heroic characters of his reformist operas *Orfeo ed Euridice*, *Alceste* and *Iphigenie* proclaimed faith in the higher qualities of the human soul and man's potential for good.

Vienna worshipped Gluck but failed to appreciate fully the significance of his innovations. Compared to the splendour and glitter of old-style *opera seria* productions the restrained dramatism of *Orfeo* and *Alceste* seemed dull. It was not until he reached Paris in the 1770s that Gluck found a really receptive and appreciative audience and dedicated supporters of his reform. In Paris, after a hard and highly-principled struggle, his views were recognised without reservation and his style of heroic musical drama, the forerunner of opera as we know it today, began its march across European stages.

Mozart who was intimately familiar with Gluck's *Orfeo* and *Alceste* was quick to appreciate the excellent prospects Gluck's reform opened up before the musical theatre of the day. And yet he stopped short of following Gluck's lead in the field of *opera seria*. He had his own aesthetic ideas to develop and to assert. Mozart used Gluck's models as a kind of spring-board—he soared higher and further. Indeed, a true comparison between Gluck and Mozart is not possible in the field of *opera seria* for fundamental reasons. For Mozart the dramatist is at his greatest not in the domain of *opera seria*, but rather in that of the Italian drama *dramma giocoso*—and this domain was completely closed to Gluck. Gluck did not have the ability to carry the action forward, in ensembles and in finales—to colour the characters with a light stroke of the brush, to invest them in a flash with sensuous reality—and that was the ability that Mozart possessed in the highest degree. Gluck's procedure was rationalistic; he presented in one aria only a single essential character trait, another in another aria and it was only the sum of these traits that yielded the complete rounded portrait. And he became a "reformer" of *opera seria* perhaps precisely because he lacked the "safety-valve" of *opera buffa*. Not so with Mozart.

Mozart had not the slightest urge to reform the opera, to change the relations between drama and music. He merely filled them with new, superior musical content. Mozart's acute insight into human nature made him as an opera composer one of the sharpest delineators of character in all music drama. It is precisely the opera that Mozart invested most with music and with an overwhelming abundance of sensuous reality expressed by means of music. And he made the aria the principal vehicle for expressing the full gamut of human emotions—jealousy, vengeance, love, hate, friendship, etc., and placed it right at the centre of his operas.

These features of Mozart's operatic art are all in evidence in *Idomeneo*. Mozart's conception of dramatic truth was different from Gluck's. For Mozart it is music that is of first importance; the poet is there only to serve the musician. The relation, the balance between drama and music with Mozart is quite different from what it is with Gluck—it is a merging into a single stream, and often the fullness of the music's power is so great that the current bears the operatic vessel along even when the action temporarily slackens and fails altogether. We will have more to say about this later in our story when we discuss *Don Giovanni*.

And yet for all its merits and strengths *Idomeneo* was not a perfect work in every respect. Seeking to bring together in harmony the achievements of different operatic schools—Italian, French, Gluckian—and to overcome the hide-bound conventions and devices of *opera seria* Mozart had not as yet developed a complete unity of style which resulted in the opera's musical language becoming somewhat heavier than was desirable. For all that it was not eclectic since Mozart's original creative genius showed through clearly, despite all the influences that were apparent.

Idomeneo was a critical success and received unqualified recognition from the connoisseurs of opera. But the majority of Munich opera goers, while expressing admiration for parts of Mozart's opera, received it coolly, on the whole. This did not discourage Mozart too much for he knew he was on the right track. *Idomeneo* was a major landmark in his entire career, it was a Rubicon. Now that he saw tangible evidence of his ability to transmute with his creative genius everything he touched, he realised the full power of his dramatic gift and inspiration and was aware of the full measure of his maturity as a composer of unique originality and consummate skill. He was no longer prepared to come to terms with his humiliating dependence on the Archbishop. The sense of rebellion which had been building up for so long was rapidly stretching his patience to breaking point. And he began looking around for a pretext to make a clean break with the Archbishop.

During his stay at Munich for the first performance of *Idomeneo* Mozart also wrote two concert arias for soprano and a quartet for oboe and strings for his friend Ramm, among other compositions.

Prince-Archbishop
Hieronymus Colloredo.

HIERONYMUS IOSEPHUS ex III:ma Prosapia
S.R.I. Princ. Colloredo de Waldsee et Mels.
eligitur die 14 Martii 1772.

While he was in the full enjoyment of the pleasures of the Carnival into which he plunged as soon as his labours were over, he suddenly received a summons from the Archbishop to join him in Vienna. He started immediately, and after a journey of four days, arrived in Vienna where he was destined to remain, except for a few short trips to nearby cities, for the rest of his life.

His first experiences in Vienna were not encouraging. He was made to live with the Archbishop's household and dine at the servants' table, treatment in striking contrast to that he received from the aristocracy in general.

Colloredo liked to appear in society with Mozart as his domestic virtuoso, but would not allow Mozart to play alone in any house but his own, or to give public recitals. The Archbishop had, however, to give in to the requests of the Viennese nobility to allow Mozart to play at concerts sponsored by the local aristocratic art society, where he scored great success. At the Archbishop's private concert later Mozart also excited considerable enthusiasm but was often addressed on that occasion by the Archbishop and his stewards as *"Gassenbube"* (street urchin). His father tried to reason with Wolfgang and urged him to forbearance, but to no avail: Wolfgang was resolved to leave a situation where he had to endure such humiliations in public. The opportunity presented itself only too soon.

The Archbishop, disliked by the nobility and by the Emperor Joseph II, was not invited to Laxenburg, the royal summer residence and, much piqued, he decided to leave Vienna. The household was to start first, but apparently Mozart was turned out of the house before the others. Feeling slighted he then took lodgings with the Webers who were in the city at the time and failed to present himself to the Archbishop when the latter expected him. At the next audience Mozart was greeted by Colloredo with terms of abuse. That was the last straw.

When he received no answer to his first request to be discharged from the Archbishop's service, Mozart drew up another memorandum and presented himself in the Archbishop's antechamber. Colloredo thought that Mozart was only bluffing, that he was looking for better terms. He did not believe that Mozart really dared to resign. Mozart had received much brutal treatment from the Archbishop and the most humiliating episode was when Count Arco, the Archbishop's high steward, insulted him and literally kicked him out of the room.

For the next few days Mozart stayed at the Webers' and became seriously ill, being close to a nervous breakdown at one point. But having overcome the psychological crisis he emerged with renewed determination and confidence. He was now ready for everything that might lie ahead of him—poverty, starvation and even death. He wrote to his father: "I shall never have anything to do with Salzburg again". And indeed Mozart never looked back. Explaining his position in the same letter he wrote that ". . . For your sake, I will sacrifice my happiness, my health and my life, but my honour, that must come before all else, both for my sake and for yours. I am convinced that the heart ennobles (*Das Herz adelt den Menschen*). I may not be of great importance yet I have a greater sense of honour than has any important position".

Thus ended the youth of Mozart and the next period of his life and career began, the period of maturity, that saw the creation of his best works which immortalised him.

Two views of Vienna by Bernardo Bellotto.

Chapter 2

Maturity

Die Entführung aus dem Serail
(The Abduction from the Seraglio)

Things were rather difficult for Mozart during his first year of freedom. He was on his own in Vienna. He had to look for lessons, to provide for his daily needs and to reestablish old contacts. Deprived of the care and support that he used to enjoy in his family, the sort of difficulties he ran into in daily life often found him at a loss. He found solace in his work whose frenetic intensity would have broken a less gifted musician. Early in the morning he would compose, then make the rounds of the homes where he gave music lessons. In the evening he would give concerts, and on reaching home would resume composing, working far into the night. His reward for his titanic labours was meagre, barely enough to make both ends meet.

Looking after his wardrobe was a particular headache for Mozart. He could not afford to appear in high society salons poorly or carelessly dressed. Then again plain cheap clothes offended his refined taste. He secretly suffered from his unprepossessing appearance and short stature and so elegant clothes seemed to him essential to improve the impression he made on other people. But Mozart's innate cheerfulness, and his resilient spirit helped him to remain optimistic.

Vienna was to play a tremendous role in Mozart's intellectual development: the broad spectrum of people of various social backgrounds he met there, their relationships and characters, the exclusive life styles of the Viennese nobility and the bourgeoisie, the life of common people which Mozart also closely observed, combined to provide rich food for thought and material in working out the imagery of his future instrumental works and his operas.

Mozart made friends quickly and he was fortunate in finding many sincere admirers in Vienna. His inborn sense of tact and good manners earned him acceptance in high society. While safeguarding his dignity, Mozart was careful not to overstep the mark in his relations with people of a higher social class. While he sought no intimacy with high-born music lovers he did not feel inferior in their company. His manner was as relaxed and simple with people of exalted rank as with his equals, members of his own class.

That was a time when revolutionary ideas, emanating from France, spread throughout the whole of Europe, exciting hopes among the lower classes and alarm and deep concern among the conservative aristocracy. A general mood of uplift and intellectual ferment prevailed in Austria as well. Emperor Joseph II even toyed with a few reformist, if utopian, ideas. In February 1781 he shared his ideas on the subject of wise and rational government with the Archbishop of Salzburg: "The state over which I rule should be guided by my fundamental principles which are: that prejudice, fanaticism, factional strife and slavery of spirit must be eliminated and all my subjects be free to exercise those freedoms which are their birthright."

How these "freedoms" worked out in practice Mozart's sad fate exemplifies. More often than not the Emperor's utopian day-dreaming was counter-productive. But a certain measure of free thinking, opposition to the hidebound ways of the nobility with their feudal prejudice, and an ironic appraisal of their tastes and traditional practices did, nevertheless, liven up the atmosphere at some of the Viennese aristocratic salons.

Revolutionary ideas found a ready response among the bourgeois intellectuals, among members of the "third estate" to which Mozart belonged. In Vienna he moved in the literary, scholarly and musical circles and felt himself attracted to actors for whom he had shown a particular fascination since his Salzburg days. In their company he was in his element.

Mozart was an extraordinarily gifted man with a keen mind and independent spirit. His judgements and comments were noted for aptness and revealed keen powers of observation. He had a philosophical turn of mind and his close association with critically-minded and outspoken people influenced the trend of his work as a composer.

A wave of national emancipation was rising among the progressive circles of Austrian society. Calls were openly made for a greater reliance on domestic creative forces and the idea was proclaimed that people had a right to develop their own art. Under pressure of these ideas Emperor Joseph II, whose own preference was for Italian opera, decided to accommodate the wishes of his people and ordered the establishment of a theatre in Vienna which would stage drama plays and musical performances in the native language. The inauguration of the *Nazional-*

The Rennweg Orhpanage in Vienna. According to Leopold, Mozart wrote some music for the orphanage choir in 1768, including a Mass and a trumpet concerto. Fragments of the Mass have come to light since the Second World War.

Vienna, a view from the gardens of Neuwaldegg Castle. Coloured engraving by Ludwig Janscha, about 1793.

Vienna, 'Am Hof.' On the left is the Collalto Palace where Wolfgang and Nannerl appeared before the Viennese nobility in 1762.

theater was a landmark event in Viennese theatrical life of the early 1780s. The problem of creating national opera had long faced German and Austrian composers and only the neglectful attitude of the ruling circles and a desperate lack of funds prevented the realisation of the long-cherished dream. Now that the opportunity of writing for the national stage presented itself Mozart was one of the first Austrian composers to find the right approach to the solution of the problem.

Within his first year in Vienna he received an operatic commission from the recently-established *Nazionaltheater*. This was an undreamt of stroke of luck.

Even during his last trip to Mannheim Mozart wrote to his father of his fervent desire to write an opera but hesitated whether he should do it in Italian, French or German style. He felt that the latter was beyond him and yet he wrote prophetically in the same letter: "How I would be loved if only I could help the German opera to its feet. And I could probably succeed." Now he was facing this very task and his awareness of this induced him to tackle it with a particular sense of responsibility.

This major development in Mozart's creative life coincided with an important change in his private life. In Vienna he again met the Webers, his old friends from Mannheim. Aloysia was engaged as prima donna in Vienna in 1780 and married Joseph Lange, the court actor. She was now a star of the Viennese stage. Her father died and in Vienna the widow, Mother Weber lived with her three daughters. She invited Mozart to lodge with them and he gladly agreed—hoping that the women would take over at least part of the more time-consuming household chores and would look after him a bit. Before long he took a fancy to eighteen-year-old Constanze, one of the daughters. Mozart's attachment to Constanze grew almost daily and she returned the feeling. He wrote to his father about his intention to marry who replied admonishing him seriously. Leopold began to feel irritated by what he saw as his son's total lack of practical common sense and he reproached Wolfgang for failing in his duty to his father. This deepened the rift that had appeared in relations between them since Wolfgang's return from Paris. All attempts at dissuasion were in vain. Mozart's resolution was fixed and on August 4, 1782, he led Constanze to the altar, against the will of Leopold and Nannerl.

Vienna, view of the Prater, one of the most popular spots in the capital and often viewed by the Emperor. Coloured engraving by Ludwig Janscha and Johann Ziegler, 1790.

Aloysia Weber (1760-1839). In October 1780 she married the actor and portrait painter Josef Lange (1751-1831), whose unfinished portrait of Mozart is one of the most famous likenesses of the composer.

Josef and Aloysia Lange. From an engraving by Daniel Berger after the drawing by Lange, 1785.

HERR UND MADAME LANGE
Mitglieder des K.k. National
Hoftheaters in Wien.

Address of a letter from Mozart to Constanze
before they were married.

Constanze, aged 17.

Marriage contract of Mozart and Constanze.

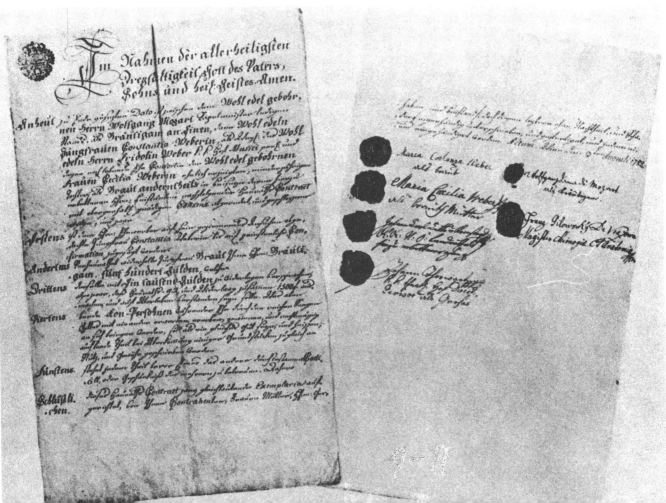

His love affair with Constanze Weber had influenced Mozart's work on the opera *The Abduction from the Seraglio*, the more so, perhaps, since the heroine had the same name as his fiancee. And Wolfgang coloured the emotional experiences of the amorous Belmonte with some of his own feeling for Constanze.

His future wife shared quite a few traits of his character. Like Wolfgang, Constanze was incapable of feigning feelings, was kind, carefree and cheerful. Like him, she overcame hardships with a light heart and had an excellent artistic temperament. Although she was not herself gifted with any great musical talent she had a pleasing, well-trained voice and was possessed of some skill on the pianoforte.

In the opera Constanze's character traits seemed to be divided between the two heroines: the lyrical Constanze and the comic Blonde. Other characters of the opera also exhibited traits which seemed to have been copied by Mozart from their real-life models. Gottlieb Stephanie, the actor who worked on the libretto had also contributed to making the characters of the opera more true to life. While he lacked any in-depth knowledge of the theory of the theatre he was a very experienced practitioner of the stage, a talented comic actor who knew well the tastes and predilections of the Viennese theater buffs.

The first Viennese musical comedies, known as Singspiels created by Mozart's predecessors were rather chaotic pastiches of Italian, French and German comedies. This fuzziness of style seemed to suit Mozart very well when he embarked on his reformist path as it enabled him to shake off the strait-jacket of Italian influences and continue experimenting on bringing different forms together in harmony, something he had tried to do in *La Finta giardiniera*.

The plot of *Die Entführung* had long been a favourite theatrical theme in Austria: the hero rescues his loved one from captivity amid a conventionally exotic setting. Several *singspiels* had been written on the libretto used by Mozart before him. But Stephanie while adapting it for Mozart cut dialogue in some places replacing it in others with duets, ariettas and ensembles. Besides, at Mozart's request, he made characters more vivid and the situations they found themselves in more natural and psychologically-motivated. Incidentally, the author of the play which Gottlieb Stephanie adapted for the libretto of Mozart's opera lodged a violent protest which was published in the *Leipziger Zeitung* for 1782: "A person in Vienna by the name of Mozart, had the audacity to misuse my drama *Belmont und Constanze* as an opera text. I must protest against this infringement of my copyright and reserve the right to take further action."

Constanze Weber (1763-1842) at about the
time of her marriage to Mozart, 1782.

Mozart in 1783.

Much in *Die Entführung* remained typical of the Italian *opera buffa*: two pairs of lovers, masters and servants, a coarse, irascible but also amorous old fool (Osmin), a number of typical situations—altercations, drunken revelry, merrymaking, the old man's philandering, a violent quarrel followed by a reconciliation of the lovers. But into this familiar setting Mozart introduced new elements and a fresh interpretation, using the possibilities of comic opera in a new way. He left all noisy and bustling scenes without music (which was allowed in a German *Singspiel*) linking the musical development with the intrinsic dynamism of the play, with character delineation and relationships between the heroes. Mozart was not put off by the rather primitive make-up of some of the characters: specific character traits whether comic, grotesque or commonplace seemed to him to be sufficiently rewarding material for his musical imagery.

At the same time Mozart sought to emphasise those characters who articulated lofty sentiments (Belmonte, Constanze) thereby gaining a greater measure of freedom in designing the structure of the opera, a wider range of emotions and an opportunity for contrasting comparisons. Because of this the comic characters in the opera came out in bold relief.

As in *La Finta giardiniera* so in *Die Entführung* Mozart again used a variety of operatic forms—*buffo* patter (Osmin's part), romance (Pedrillo's romance), a lyrical song with virtuoso elements of the "seria" aria (Constanze's part). He also found rewarding material in the aria of the so-called "intermediate" kind (*semiseria*, i.e. half-serious)—it is here that Mozart's *national spirit* and innovative approach fully came into their own. This kind of aria is typified by Constanze's first monologue expressing her homesickness, and more particularly, by Belmonte's aria which opens the opera. Belmonte's lyrical theme is free of the conventional histrionics usually associated with *opera seria*. It sounds like real human conversation with its characteristic excitement and fitful rhythm. The accentuation of the melody and its development freely follow the meaning and sound of the opera text. Even coloratura, as used by Mozart, has none of its usual character of florid vocal embellishment, but is instead organically integrated into the structure of the melody thereby emphasising Belmonte's excited and concerned state of mind. The transition from elevated high-flown intonations to commonplace, or lyrical ones, occurs as simply and naturally as in normal human speech. All this stood in stark contrast to the declaratory, histrionic manner adopted by the Italian *opera seria* which froze the expression of human emotions and sentiment in an immutable conventionalised mould.

Die Entführung thus exhibited early signs of the reform of the

Kimberley Potts

Ms. Fusconi

College English 12, Period 4

15, April 1996

Thesis: Mozart was a child prodigy of music, who
was a highly gifted child, that excited admiration
and wonder in music.

Define Prod.   talk/write

I. Mozart's younger years.

A. Mozart's accomplishments at the age of three.

B. Mozart's talents at the age of four.

II. Mozart growing up.

A. Mozart at age five.

B. Mozart at age six.

C. Mozart at age seven.

D. Mozart at age eight.

III The adolescent Mozart.

A. Mozart's accomplishments and capabilities

B. Some of Mozarts talents and skills.

Blonde's aria 'Welche Wonne, welche Lust' from *Il Seraglio*. Autograph facsimile (Tübingen, Universitätsbibliothek).

operatic language which subsequently gained tremendous momentum and effected a historic change in the art of opera. By tearing down the compartmentalization of opera dictated by convention which separated the musical speech of *opera seria* from the ordinary intonations of *opera buffa* Mozart moved opera closer to today's theatrical realism. The results of this reform fed the work of several generations of composers.

While revolutionising the language of opera Mozart, at the same time, sought to make isolated operatic forms part of the overall development of the action, to confer on the music clearly-defined scenic outlines. An example of this is Pedrillo's romance which he sings in the garden at night to let the prisoners of the Pasha, Constanze and her confidante Blonde, know that Belmonte and his ship are ready for an escape that night. The librettist originally intended to have here a light number, say, a serenade, but Mozart read the dramatic meaning of the scene differently: the music of the romance that he wrote embodies the lovers' mood of alarm, the sombre colour of the night sky, the uneasy caution and a feeling of tense anticipation.

111

Mozart at the Berlin performance of *The Abduction from the Seraglio*.

The comedy aria offered ample new opportunities for doing so. Despite his lyrical predilections Mozart, already in *Die Ent-fuhrung*, seemed to know just which operatic form he would use as the mainstay of his reform. He worked towards this reform proceeding from realist trends emerging in the German version of comic opera rather than from the conventionality of the ex-alted theatricality of the Italian *opera seria*.

Already the overture to *Die Entfuhrung* demonstrates Mo-zart's dramatic gift and sense of theatre. The overture is full of boisterous, cheerful brilliant music which immediately puts the audience right in the middle of the exotic atmosphere of the op-era. Mozart ingeniously included in the orchestra instruments that helped him create "Turkish music": piccolo, trumpets and timpani, triangle and cymbals. And what colour they lend to the Overture, to the Janissary choruses, to Osmin's outburst of anger—a colouration at once exotic, gay, and menacing. The middle part of the Overture which generalises the lyrical elements of the play, contains an innovation: Mozart anticipates the appearance of his hero on the stage by making the orchestra narrate Belmonte's aria.

True, neither in the Overture nor in the overall design of the opera does Mozart achieve the full organic fusion of the various forms. Certain types of aria exist side by side without merging and even introducing a certain discord in the character delineation. Belmonte's last aria is rationalistic written in the spirit of *opera seria* and contrasts with his first two characteristic arias. In his efforts to convey the complexity and multi-dimensionality of the relationships among the heroes Mozart does not as yet avoid slipping up on the contradiction of style. On the other hand, in conveying the straightforward emotional experiences of Osmin, Pedrillo, Blonde, he achieves complete unity of music and drama. By combining German folk melodies with the character quality of the *buffa* devices Mozart created full blooded, realistic characters. Subsequently, he would have to divest them of the conventionality of grotesque, to make them more complex and noble.

An Ottoman Janissary band of the kind that inspired 'Turkish music' and 'Turkish' themes throughout the 18th and early 19th centuries. The sound of these instruments influenced not only Mozart but also Gluck and Haydn, as well as Beethoven in his Ninth Symphony. A plate from *Les anciens costumes de l'Empire Ottoman* by Arif Pasa (Paris, 1864).

Mozart in 1780.

Chapter 3

Instrumental Works of the Vienna Period

Le Nozze di Figaro (The Marriage of Figaro)

Four years separate *Die Entfuhrung* from the appearance of *The Marriage of Figaro*. These years Mozart lived the hectic life of an artist, working at full stretch and at the same time enjoying life with an avidity and *joie de vivre* which were characteristic of him throughout his life. These years saw his virtuoso talents reach their acme. No one could dispute Mozart's preeminence as a harpsichordist. He had competed against some of the world's best-known harpsichord players and won. The famous London virtuoso Muzio Clementi was lost in admiration for the freedom of Mozart's brilliant improvisations and the irresistible charm of his playing, at once inspired and austere, with the most delicate iridescence of shades and colours of sound. During these years Mozart seemed to have recaptured some of his former glory. In a letter to his father describing his daily routine he enclosed a schedule of his concerts for weeks ahead which gives an idea of the sheer physical strain they imposed on him, a strain that would have broken any lesser musician than Mozart. He played almost daily, sometimes twice a day both at public concerts and at his own "academies"—musical gatherings at which the composer's works in a variety of forms were performed, at chamber concerts, at aristocratic salons, and public contests with outstanding virtuosos. All these followed in quick succession.

The only thing that remained closed to him was official recognition on which Mozart's material well-being largely de-

115

Antonio Salieri
(1750-1825), friend of
Haydn and Beethoven,
enemy of Mozart.

Muzio Clementi
(1746-1832), composer,
pianist and music
publisher. He settled in
London in 1798.
Engraving by J. Niedl
after Thomas Hardy.

The Marriage of Figaro Autograph facsimile of a page from Act III, sc. viii. The manuscript, originally in the Preussische Staatsbibliothek, Berlin, disappeared in 1945.

pended. Emperor Joseph II never evinced an intention to give him a more or less important musical appointment at court. The palace was an artistic citadel jealously guarded by a handful of musicians who had been accepted by the royal family. Among those in particular favour at the time were Christoph Gluck, the venerable master known for his independence and generally held in high esteem, and Antonio Salieri, the energetic and experienced Italian operatic and church composer who had quickly made his mark. Gluck took a lively interest in Mozart whose *Die Entfuhrung* drew his flattering comments. But a series of strokes put the aging composer outside the mainstream of musical and social life and there was nothing he could do for Mozart. Salieri remained the music "master" at court. His relations with Mozart, at first outwardly friendly, soon degenerated into a hidden deep-running animosity based perhaps on that painful jealousy and envy on the part of a talented musician for one of genius which Pushkin described with such tremendous poetic power in his little tragedy *Mozart and Salieri*. Be that as it may, Salieri saw to it that Mozart was kept well outside the ambit of life at court.

In this period, when Mozart's talents were in full flower and he was at the peak of his powers, he did not as yet react to the unappreciative attitude of the court as painfully as he did later. Recognition by the entire clique of courtiers meant infinitely less to him than his friendship with Joseph Haydn. The celebrated Viennese symphonist, then at the zenith of his fame, was perhaps the only musician of rank who saw Mozart's creative genius for what it was. In a conversation with Mozart's father Haydn said: "I declare to you before God . . . that your son is the greatest composer that I know; he has taste, and . . . the most consummate knowledge of the art of composition." In return for this avowal Mozart dedicated to Haydn six quartets. "It is but his due," Mozart said, "for from Haydn I first learnt how to compose a quartet."

The friendship of the two great artists one of whom was a full quarter of a century younger than the other left a profound mark on the work of both. The original and intensely national genius of Haydn and the remarkable perfection of his works often illuminated the way for Mozart as he made his own discoveries in the art of composition. Thus in response to Haydn's six quarters Mozart wrote six quartets of his own in which the individual characteristics of his creative genius are refracted through the features he shared with Haydn.

For his part, Haydn, too, came under the influence of Mozart's singular gift. The works of his younger friend enabled him to discover and explore a new world of sentiment and conceptions characteristic of the younger generation which until then had been closed to Haydn. His last symphonies, completed after Mozart's death, show how deeply the dramatic features of Mozart's works had penetrated Haydn's soul, as well as his commitment to a life-asserting philosophy which made Mozart the immediate predecessor of Beethoven.

Mozart's instrumental compositions written in this period are all stamped with an exciting and modern attitude to life—harpsichord concertos, sonatas, fantasias, chamber music are dominated by the six quartets Mozart dedicated to Haydn.

The profusion of works for harpsichord was a direct result of Mozart's intensive concert activity. He would play new compositions almost at every public recital amazing his audience with the inexhaustible power of his inspiration. Variations, harpsichord concertos and improvisations continued to be his favourite forms on the concert stage, along with a clavier sonata in G which soon became a leading number in his concert repertoire.

At the time the sonata form lacked well-defined outlines and its various types were still unstable. Haydn wrote two- and three-movement clavier sonatas. Mozart made the three-movement sonata his firm choice. As interpreted by him, the sonata

Dedication page of the Haydn quartets.

Al mio caro Amico Haydn

Un Padre, avendo risolto di mandare i suoi figlj nel gran
Mondo, stimò doverli affidare alla protezione, e condotta
d'un Uomo molto celebre in allora, il quale per buona sorte,
era di più il suo migliore Amico. — Eccoti dunque del pari,
Uom celebre, ed Amico mio carissimo i sei miei figlj. — Essi sono,
è vero il frutto di una lunga, è laboriosa fatica, pur la speranza
fattami da più Amici di vederla almeno in parte compensata,
m'incoraggisce, e mi lusinga, che questi parti siano per essermi
un giorno di qualche consolazione. — Tu stesso Amico carissimo,
nell'ultimo tuo Soggiorno in questa Capitale, me ne dimostrasti
la tua soddisfazione. — Questo tuo suffragio mi anima sopra
tutto, perché io te li raccommandi, e mi fa sperare, che non ti
sembreranno del tutto indegni del tuo favore. — Piacciati dunque
accoglierli benignamente, ed esser loro Padre, Guida, ed Amico!
Da questo momento, Io ti cedo i miei diritti sopra di essi: ti
supplico però di guardare con indulgenza i difetti, che l'occhio
parziale di Padre mi può aver celati, e di continuar loro
malgrado, la generosa tua Amicizia a chi tanto l'apprezza,
mentre sono di tutto Cuore.

Amico Carissimo   il tuo sincerissimo Amico
Vienna il p.mo Settembre 1785.
                                                        W. A. Mozart

SEI
QUARTETTI
PER DUE VIOLINI, VIOLA, E VIOLONCELLO.
Composti e Dedicati
al Signor
GIUSEPPE HAYDN
Maestro di Cappella di S. A.
il Principe d'Esterhazy &c &c
Dal Suo Amico
W. A. MOZART
Opera X.
In Vienna presso Artaria Comp.
Mercanti ed Editori di Stampa Musica,
e Carte Geografiche.

Mozart's six great quartets dedicated to Haydn and
published as his Op. 10. The engraved title page of
the original edition, 1785.

Mozart and Haydn.

Joseph Haydn.

for the first time acquired the completeness of expression which later made it a worthy rival of the harpsichord concerto. Above all this applies to the bold-relief texture of its thematic material. Even beside Haydn's themes Mozart's had striking depth and significance. Mozart's love of a singing, flexible melody constituted, in the period of his maturity, the enchanting intimacy of his harpsichord style; any of his passages resembled, in terms of the smoothness and iridescence of sound, the vocal coloratura. The famous Mozartian "singing allegro", the fast, lively movement of sonatas and concertos, excited and moved even inexperienced music lovers by their combination of impetuous tempo and the lyrical message of the melodic material.

Contact with the audience was an essential condition for Mozart the performer. Even in his early childhood he would refuse to play if he noticed that his hearers did not listen carefully enough. Now that he was at the height of his powers, the enthusiasm of the audience and its response and appreciation were still his highest reward, incomparable in value with the financial success of his concerts. As he wrote to his father after a concert in Vienna in April 1781 when he was still in the Archbishop's service: "What made me feel happy, and surprised me most,

Beethoven, about 1787.

Ludwig van Beethoven
(1770-1827), silhouette attributed
to Neesen, about 1786-87 (Bonn,
Beethoven-Haus).

was the unusual, dead silence broken in the middle of my play by sudden cries of "bravo' . . ."

Mozart was always careful to ensure that his compositions were accessible, in the good sense of the term, and really popular but never at the expense of the standard of his ideas and philosophical content of his work. He never sacrificed that, never conceded anything on that point. Far from wishing "to play up" to the audience he was always in full control, masterfully compelling the audience to follow him. Evidence of this is provided by the gradual evolution of the harpsichord concerto in Mozart's work.

The virtuoso brilliance and exquisiteness which are such a striking feature of Mozart's works for the concert stage are comparable to sublime poetry. A profound message and refined lyrical quality caused Mozart's imagery to have an unprecedented emotional impact on the audience. But in the D minor and C minor concertos, his most significant concertos written in 1785-1786, Mozart discovers a completely new area—that of dramatic concerto music, which was subsequently finally conquered by Beethoven.

Not surprisingly, the D minor concerto was perhaps the only "alien" concerto which Beethoven performed publicly: both the ideological message and the media of expression undoubtedly anticipated significant aspects of Beethoven's revolutionary thinking. The former "galant" virtuoso contest between orchestra and soloist is resolved by Mozart in terms of a stark dramatic contrast. The unusually austere, even sombre, quality of the opening orchestral theme is contrasted with the soloist's theme representative of that type of flexible, excited expressiveness of melody which is almost speech-like and so characteristic of Mozart's lyrical heroes from the time of *Die Entführung*. Thus from the opening pages of the concerto the conflict between the masterful objective dimension and the personal dimension, now protesting, now persuading, now trusting and joyously confiding in the listener, comes into its own.

Accordingly, the form of the concerto undergoes change with the result that instead of the short development typical of Mozart's earlier works in this form, which were essentially a string of virtuoso passages, Mozart introduces real symphonic development which in terms of its significance is equivalent to its framing movements—the exposition and the reprise. The whole structure of the concerto, the contrasting comparison of its movements and the contrast-based unity of the sonority of orchestra and harpsichord are dominated by an effective strength of feeling and striving towards a romantic freedom of musical thought.

In even more concentrated form these features are present in Mozart's harpsichord fantasias. In 1785 thanks to his acquaintance with Baron van Swieten who had an excellent library, Mozart familiarised himself with the works of Bach and Handel and developed a keen interest in improvisations. His attention was again attracted by those solemn majestic instrumental forms which were popular early in the 18th century and later superseded by the sonata form. Mozart tried to write with great enthusiasm in the spirit of the old classics—gigues, fugues, fantasias, endeavouring to adapt for clavier the colorful devices characteristic of the organ compositions of his predecessors. Among Mozart's experiments in "modernising" the old music forms, his fantasias stand out on account of their scale, vividness and concerto-like scope. In the fantasia in C minor which preceded another sonata in the same tonality Mozart's methods and devices of composition go beyond the possibilities of the clavier anticipating, as it were, the future works for the piano: the deep chord sonority, coloristic devices, virtuoso technique designed to convey dynamic contrasts, the theatrically vivid change of images (the prelude character of the first movement, the arioso-like character of the middle episodes and the almost scenic decorativeness of the rapid virtuoso elements). The new harmonic language, so unusual for the time, coupled with the features we have just mentioned, could not be in sharper contrast to the courtly and staid style of Mozart's earlier harpsichord compositions and marked a new stage in his creative career.

This shift brought about a fundamental change in Mozart's attitude to contemporary composers and music lovers. It turned out that in opera, too, his thinking proved (to be) too bold and too realist even for those who expressed admiration for his consummate skill as a performer. The Emperor Joseph II was reported to have said after the first performance of *Die Entfuhrung* on 16 July 1782: "Too beautiful for our ears, my dear Mozart, and far too many notes." Mozart answered frankly: "Exactly as many notes as are required, your Majesty."

But it was Mozart's chamber music, his brilliant quartets, that generated the greatest controversy.

"These barbarians with no ear for real music presumptuously think that it is music they compose," the Italian composer Sarti who worked in Vienna at the time was reported to have commented, with undisguised contempt, on the work of Mozart and some other Viennese composers.

In those days chamber music was intended to be performed at private concerts with their concentrated intimate atmosphere. Mozart knew he had a right to expect from his hearers maxi-

Joseph II, right, and his brother (later Leopold II) as young men. Detail from a painting by Pompeo Batoni (Vienna Kunsthistorisches Museum).

mum attention to his ideas and intentions. Indeed, in no other forms of music do we find such completely relaxed freedom of composition, such unusually structured and exciting themes, such complex pattern of development and radiant harmony as are present in his quartets.

The Holy Roman Emperor Leopold II.

Engraving of the Emperor
Leopold's coronation.

Here Mozart displayed with particular brilliance his innate penchant for polyphony, as well as his profound knowledge of the art of counterpoint, qualities which had gained him the membership of the Bologna Academy of Music when he was still a twelve-year-old boy. The independent development of voices coupled with the free flow of several melodies formed the basis of the quartet style of the mature Mozart. The most refined and delicate polyphonic development which charmed him so much in Haydn's quartets received a new interpretation in the hands of Mozart. Whereas Haydn liked to divide up a theme into individual motives and then proceeded to develop its components to create lively exchanges between voices, Mozart saw melody as an integral whole, a sum total of its expressive means. Far from wishing to split up his theme he preferred to give, in several voices, a combination of independent and often structurally dissimilar melodies (this device was later frequently used by the Romantics).

This type of unification of melodies resulted in new and, at times, sharply discordant, subtle and refined new chord combinations whose exquisite character often caused the displeasure of Mozart's high-born clients. Even those admirers of his talent who were particularly friendly to him sometimes complained about the extraordinary complexity of his ensemble music. In

Early 19th century set for *La Clemenza di Tito,* originally produced in Prague, 6 September 1791, to mark the coronation of Leopold II as King of Bohemia.

LA CLEMENZA
DI TITO,
DRAMMA SERIO PER MUSICA
IN DUE ATTI
DA RAPPRESENTARSI
NEL TEATRO NAZIONÁLE
DI PRAGA
NEL SETTEMBRE 1791.
IN OCCASIONE DI SOLLENIZZARE
IL GIORNO DELL' INCORONAZIONE
DI SUA
MAESTA L'IMPERATORE
LEOPOLDO II.

NELLA STAMPERIA DI MOB. DE SCHÖNFELD.

Title page of the libretto
at the premiere of *La Clemenza di Tito.*

Manuscript from the opera
La Clemenza di Tito.

fact, one of his patrons during a rehearsal of Mozart's latest quartets impatiently crossed out some of the parts assuming that their bold sound was the result of the copyist's carelessness.

It took considerable confidence in his powers, an independence of mind and great forbearance for Mozart to swim against the current of opinion of the very people on whose support his welfare and future as a composer hinged. But when it came to defending his innovations and new approaches, which he saw as absolutely essential, Mozart was adamant and had the courage of his convictions. He could really put up a fight and win.

The deep-seated ideological conflict between the great artist and his exalted patrons, the first signs of which emerged in his youth, was slowly but inexorably becoming more apparent. True, it was not until later that Mozart began to feel the full perilous consequences of this conflict. What kept him out of trouble between 1782 and 1786 was his unsurpassed virtuosity and the reputation of being Austria's best harpsichordist. Then again his intensive concert performances maintained his optimism. Awareness of his creative powers made him feel happy and helped him to overcome the hardships of his precarious existence with a light heart. An indefatigable worker, he still found time for relaxation and simple pleasures. His friends were among the cream of the Viennese artistic community and the Mozarts often kept open house. His modest home was always full of guests and resounded with merry laughter and jokes.

At one of the parties given at his house Mozart met a man who was to play an important part in his subsequent evolution as operatic composer. He was Lorenzo da Ponte, real name Emmanuele Conegliano, the Emperor's court poet. The son of an impoverished Italian Jew, he was adopted as a boy and baptised by a church dignitary. A literary man of some note, at one time he held a professorship at Treviso University but after a series of quarrels, followed by politically-coloured adventures, had to flee Italy and settled in Vienna. His main occupation in the imperial capital was to supply librettos for operas chosen and commissioned by the Emperor. In due course, da Ponte became a well known dramatist of considerable dramatic and poetic talent. But everything he did for other composers was fairly run-of-the-mill. It was not until he met Mozart and appreciated his unique genius that da Ponte's own talent began to unfold to the full.

Mozart was deeply impressed with da Ponte's bold, shrewd and observant wit, his tremendous experience and his ironic attitude to the conventions of life in the Holy Roman Empire at

Lorenzo da Ponte
(1749-1838).

the time. When a few years later, in 1785, he was commissioned to write an opera for an Italian troupe which had returned to the Viennese stage he found the idea of joining forces with da Ponte attractive.

By then Mozart's operatic aesthetics had become a mature and highly original phenomenon.

His views on the opera differed from those of Gluck who recognised the primacy of drama over music. Mozart, in contrast, took the opposite view believing music to be the heart of the dramatic design of any opera. In a 1782 letter to his father, while working on *Die Entfuhrung*, he wrote: "In an opera the poetry must be the obedient daughter of the music." Mozart followed this principle unswervingly while striving at the same time, like Gluck, to achieve an organic fusion between drama and music.

A born theatrical composer, Mozart judged operatic material on its theatrical merit and stageability. His musical images stemmed directly from those outlined by the libretto. They

Johann Nepomuk Hummel (1778-1837). An anonymous portrait in oils (Vienna, Gesellschaft der Musikfreunde). Hummel started playing the clavier at the age of four, became a pupil of Mozart at the age of eight (in 1876) and later was a famous composer, pianist and teacher.

were closely bound up with the plot while at the same time had an independent musical and scenic life to live. By revealing the essence of the play's central conflict, the inner, psychological line of its action, to project the main idea of the play to the audience better, Mozart recreated, as it were, the dramatic basis of his works for the theatre.

This distinctive feature shaped Mozart's approach to traditional operatic forms. Like Gluck, he sought to overcome the disjointed, mixed character of the traditional structure of opera. But unlike Gluck, who in an effort to avoid the independent significance of arias, their concert virtuoso quality made the dramatic recitative the basis of his reform, Mozart drew on the entire wealth of the operatic heritage to do what he wanted. By boldly transmuting traditional forms to give them a fresh interpretation he was able to bring out their theatrical potential. The aria and the ensemble remained for Mozart the pivotal points of his style of operatic composition but the aria only as a means of character delineation, while the ensemble as a vehicle for conveying the overall composition of the characters so as to emphasize the contrast between them, or else to expose the psychological connection.

Mozart's persistent searchings as he strove to reform the conventional operatic forms and language produced refreshingly new and unexpected results as evidenced not only by *Idomeneo* and *Die Entführung* but also by the little elegant Singspiel *Der Schauspiel-Director*, written between the completion of *Die Entführung* and the first production of *Figaro*, and even by *L'Oca del Cairo (The Goose of Cairo)*, a series of unfinished operatic scenes to an eccentric plot in which Mozart was soon disappointed.

After receiving the commission Mozart looked through dozens of librettos in search of a suitable plot which would give him inspiration or at least be suitable for subsequent adaptation. But nothing he saw fired his imagination. Psychologically, he had long gone beyond the confines of traditional operatic techniques, the standard of operatic dramaturgy prevailing at the time, and everything he looked at seemed pathetic and substandard for his purposes. Then one day Mozart suggested to da Ponte that they should adapt their work from Beaumarchais, whose play *Le Marriage de Figaro* was famous throughout Europe. After making quite a stir following its first performance in Paris in 1784 it became the object of heated public debate. At first it was received with admiration by all the sections of Parisian society including the royal family. But its true revolutionary message soon became apparent and was not lost on the upper classes who became quite incensed.

Other librettists had been attracted by Beaumarchais's controversial play and three operas had already been staged at Vienna's *Burgtheater*, all dealing with the troubled relationships between different classes. None of them, however, even began to measure up to Mozart's version.

Rumours of the play's social edge and bite reached the ears of most European rulers who took a dim view of it. The Emperor banned it from the Austrian stage. But da Ponte promised Mozart that he would somehow obtain the Emperor's consent to have it staged as an opera in Vienna. For reasons of prudence da Ponte had to drop most of the obvious French political allusions, so that the work began to resemble Italian opera. But

Program of the first performance of *The Marriage of Figaro*. This opera was presented at the express command of the Emperor on the 1st of May 1786 at the Court Theater in Vienna.

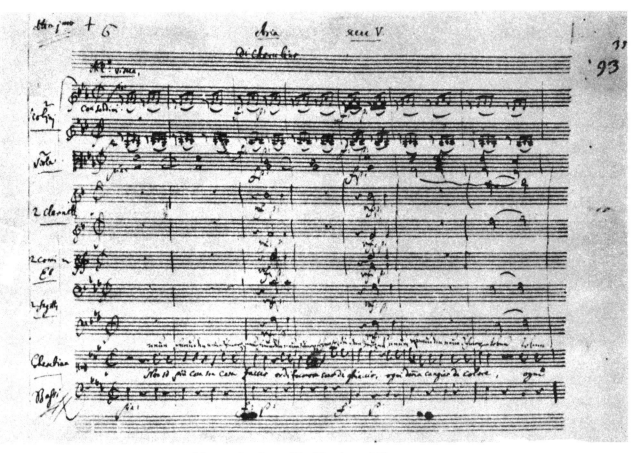

Manuscript from *The Marriage of Figaro*.

here and there he emphasised the satirical purpose with a few sharp and biting references.

While da Ponte had, understandably, to compromise so as not to offend fashionable society Mozart had no such inhibitions. The characters of Beaumarchais seemed to feel and suffer as he did, and so he used them as a mouthpiece to express his own sense of resentment and disenchantment. The bitter and ironic tone of this self-revelation was not to the liking of the less perceptive sections of Viennese society. Even so the first performances of *Le Nozze di Figaro* were a huge success.

The principle themes of *The Marriage of Figaro* are love and duty; and in the characters of Almaviva and Figaro two conflicting forces at work in eighteenth-century society are reflected—the aristocracy, stoutly committed to the status quo, and the third estate (to which Mozart himself belonged) soon to take over power. The analysis of the inner world of the charac-

The room in which
Mozart wrote *The
Marriage of Figaro*.

ters, only hinted at by da Ponte, is fully realised by Mozart in
his masterly score and perhaps nowhere more convincingly than
in the part of the Countess.

Le Nozze di Figaro was premiered after violent intrigues at
Vienna's Burgtheater on May 1, 1786. The theatre was crowded
and the audience enthusiastic; several numbers, notably ensemble passages, were repeated, others sung as many as three times,
and this went on at subsequent performances till the Emperor
Joseph II banned encores.

Having abandoned the traditional conventionalized treatment
of comedy characters, a device he had freely used in *Die Entfuhrung*, in *Le Nozze di Figaro* Mozart successfully got rid of the
pompous theatricality to achieve a more incisive delineation of
the lyrical characters of the play. As a result, all real-life situations as presented in his new opera were now in organic unity.

Thus Mozart's predilection for psychological observation, which he had displayed even as a youth, was now firmly rooted in a mature realist conception.

Although the lyrical colouring had dominated Mozart's earlier operas, in *Figaro*, thanks to the unity of musical language and character delineation, it took on the significance of a poetic idea and, as well as integrating the characters, altered the relative importance of each to the action of the opera.

Mozart worked on his innovations in *Figaro* on his own, for the most part. His musical interpretations and treatment of characters and convolutions of the plot transformed, often in unexpected ways for da Ponte, the compositional significance of individual scenes and the meaning of relationships among the characters.

The Marriage of Figaro marked a new era in the history of opera: the age of lyrical comedy when the accretions of various operatic forms and the traditional elements of each came together in an interesting and effective combination.

As in his earlier operas so in *Figaro*, Mozart concentrated the key elements of musical development in large ensembles—in *terzetti*, quartets and sextets, to make them the focal point of conflict situations and focus the attention of the audience less on the external actions of the heroes and more on the escalation and *denouement* of psychological situations. Naturally, the line which originated in *Idomeneo* and, more especially, in *Die Entführung* reaches its culmination in the finales lending a sense of fusion and completeness to the entire work. Not only in the finale of the second act, where the action is presented as a steady build-up of psychological tension followed by a sudden change (the Count's jealous suspicions, the alarm of the Countess and Susanna, the Count's disappointment in failing to surprise Cherubino, the reconciliation of the couple, and a fresh eruption of suspicion, etc.) but even in the finale of the fourth act—the night scene in the garden—where the text is based on purely external clashes of the heroes. Mozart built the musical development around the psychological moments to achieve unity between the mood dominating the various scenes and their intrinsic significance.

The Overture to Figaro for the first time in operatic history was a symphonic work in its own right, completely self-contained and clearly defined. An overture such as this could only have resulted from the perfectly organic structure of the opera as a generalisation of its theatrical and musical concept. The overture reflects the opera's external dynamism and its radiant lyricism. At the same time it serves as a means of symphonic characterisation of the play's main heroes.

Le Nozze di Figaro, then, is remarkable not only for its scope, the vividness and diversity of its material but also for its perfect form, the integrity of its overall concept and the generalising power of its message. The easy grace and fullness with which these qualities manifested themselves in Mozart's operatic masterpiece were until then a quality of the instrumental music of the great masters of the age. For this reason, *Le Nozze di Figaro* can by rights take its place beside them as a classic.

Don Giovanni. The Last Symphonies

Mozart's striking achievements could not have gone unnoticed by his contemporaries. Even *Die Entführung aus dem Serail* generated a good deal of controversy and made Mozart a favourite with the connoisseurs. Singers, orchestral musicians and conductors were quick to appreciate what excellent new prospects Mozart's reform of the opera opened up before them. A modest composer who had never been in favour at court gained unqualified recognition from his brothers in art. In effect, Mozart was educating a new generation of operatic performers by introducing them to new realist techniques in the treatment of opera characters. His intimate knowledge of the theatre and vocal music and technique made the newness of Mozart's imagery particularly attractive to the performers. Mozart never violated the nature of the vocalist. By offering an opportunity for a wider and more intelligent application of virtuoso techniques Mozart introduced the singer to his reform of the musical language gently, exercising great caution. The rehearsals of Mozart's operas often developed into triumphs for the composer. The full orchestra dress rehearsal of *Figaro* was no exception.

Describing Mozart conducting his new opera the Irish tenor Michael Kelly who took the parts of Basilio and Don Curzio later wrote with great enthusiasm: "Never was anything more complete than the triumph of Mozart, and his 'Le Nozze di Figaro', to which numerous overflowing audiences bore witness. Even at the first full orchestra rehearsal, all those present were roused to enthusiasm, and when Benucci came to the fine passage, '*Cherubino, alla vittoria, alla gloria militar*', which he gave with stentorian lungs, the effect was electrifying, for the whole of the performers on the stage, and those in the orchestra, as if actuated by one feeling of delight, cried with one voice '*Bravo, Maestro! Viva, viva, grande Mozart!*' Those in the orchestra I thought would never have ceased applauding, by beating the bows of their violins against the music desks."*

And what of Mozart?

Kelly continued: "I never shall forget his little animated face when lighted up with the glowing rays of genius;—it is impossible to describe it, as it would be to paint sun beams."**

Discerning admirers of Mozart's genius immediately saw what a revolutionary opera *The Marriage of Figaro* was. They bore witness to the musical embodiment of living people, with complex inner lives linked together by the unity of action, thought and mood. It was, indeed, the dawn of a new era in the history of opera.

The Viennese public received *Figaro* with a warm enthusiasm that surprised and touched Mozart. But the general kow-towing to the Emperor's tastes, who had never been a Mozart admirer, soon made itself felt. In due course, unflattering comments from "on high" dampened the excitement and interest which the first production of *Figaro* had generated. Instead, a skeptical, fault-finding attitude to Mozart's innovations to which Vienna had not yet become accustomed, prevailed. After a brief run with fair financial success *Figaro* disappeared from the Viennese stage, as did *Die Entfuhrung* before it.

The year 1786, when *The Marriage of Figaro* appeared, also saw a strange cooling off of the public towards Mozart the concert performer. After a period of frequent public and private concerts when he was literally bombarded with invitations Mozart was gradually being ousted from this area of musical life. Pleading changed circumstances, his former friends and admirers among the Viennese nobility stopped commissioning Mozart to write compositions for the concert stage.

As in previous years, in 1786 Mozart had an idea to announce his own "academies", i.e. subscription concerts given by the composer at his own (financial) risk. But their financial return depended on the amount aristocratic music lovers and patrons were willing to subscribe. In former years Mozart would need but a few such concerts to secure the sum he hoped to raise. This time, however, the list of subscribers contained just one name, that of the long-time patron of many Austrian musicians—Baron Gottfried van Swieten. Mozart's last hope of improving his pecuniary condition was thus dashed. Meantime his expenses were mounting: the birth of successive children, Con-

---

*M. Kelly: 'Reminiscences', I, 262.

**Ibid., I, 258, 259.

Vienna, the Michaelplatz and the Burgtheater where *Figaro* was first performed on 1 May 1786. The *Seraglio* was also performed here in 1782, and *Cosi fan tutte* was to be premiered in 1790. Coloured engraving, anonymous.

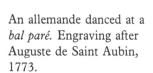

An allemande danced at a *bal paré*. Engraving after Auguste de Saint Aubin, 1773.

Vienna, the concert hall in the Augarten. Coloured engraving by L. Poratsky.

Michael Kelly, Irish singer.

stanze's frequent and prolonged illnesses, and Mozart's own exhaustion and ill-health required expenditure of considerable funds. And the sources of income were dwindling. Mozart had long been running into debt. This humiliating dependence on others offended his sense of dignity. Many of his creditors exploited his desperate financial situation and imposed crippling terms on him. He had to sell the brilliant works that were issuing from his fluent pen for a pittance. Music publishing in those days was in its infancy and compositions were duplicated primarily by copyists and Mozart frequently found himself the victim of swindlers. Under pressure of mounting debts Mozart had to abandon comfortable quarters and move into increasingly inferior apartments. Often he found himself facing impossible working conditions. What saved him and his family in those days was his inexhaustible cheerfulness and a certain carefree attitude to the vicissitudes of everyday life which his wife fully shared. But, of course, the bitter experience of a precarious existence was beginning to take its toll and Mozart found it increasingly difficult to give himself up to the simple joys of life with a wholeheartedness that was typical of him in former years. *The Marriage of Figaro* was Mozart's last tribute to his former enthusiasm for the happy and joyful side of art. The following year, 1787-1788, set a sharp demarcation line in Mozart's life. That year he wrote *Don Giovanni*.

Don Giovanni was the fruit of the success *Figaro* had enjoyed in Prague. The Bohemian capital with its high standard of musical culture, had long admired Mozart as one of its favourites. *Figaro* had a tremendous success on the Prague stage. Even *Die Entfuhrung aus dem Serail* had reached Prague not long after its first Vienna performance. In December 1786, only months behind Vienna, the Prague public enjoyed *Figaro* in a production by the Bondini Company and gave it a reception such as no other opera had ever had.

At the Vienna premiere of *Figaro* the Italian singers attempted to sabotage Mozart's music by deliberately singing false notes. The Emperor Joseph II had to intervene personally and see that the scandal was not repeated. All the more significant was the success of *Figaro* in Prague. An eyewitness, F. X.

Mozart at the Piano.
Detail from an unfinished oil on canvas by Mozart's brother-in-law, Josef Lange, about 1782-83.

Niemtschek described it thus: ". . . This opera was performed without a break throughout the whole winter. The enthusiasm it excited among the public was unprecedented. Figaro's songs were to be heard in the streets, in the gardens, and even the harp player in the local tap-room had to twang out *Non piu andrai* if he wanted people to listen". After the *Marriage of Figaro* everybody wanted to see and welcome Mozart. Count Joseph Thun invited Mozart and his wife to Prague, offering to provide them with every comfort and accommodation in his own house. Mozart was pleased to accept. Things were not going well with him and the spectre of want was never far off: the invitation to Prague was like a ray of hope.

At midday, on January 11, 1787, Mozart arrived in Prague. The newspapers wrote in great detail about his visit and the general public was expectant and excited. And Mozart himself? In the palaces below the Prague Castle, there was so much warmth, such friendly smiles, such admiration! On the day of his arrival, he attended, in the company of Count Canal, a ball given by Baron Bretfeld. Here Mozart had the first proof of the success of his music in Prague. Melodies from *Figaro* were played, arranged as "Country-dances" and "German dances". In a letter to his friend Gottfried von Jacquin, Mozart wrote: ". . . Here in Prague nothing else is talked about but Figaro, nothing is played, trumpeted, sung or whistled but Figaro, nobody goes to any other opera but Figaro, and only Figaro—undoubtedly a great honour for me".

When Mozart left Prague a month later he had with him a new contract from Bondini's company for another opera. The fee was generous—100 ducats. The terms of the contract were most favourable. The choice of the libretto was up to Mozart. After making rough drafts in Vienna he was expected in Prague later in the year to complete the opera in the city.

The offer could not have come at a better time for Mozart. It gave him a welcome respite from his financial worries and he could now devote himself wholly to creative work. Da Ponte hit upon the popular story of Don Juan for the libretto probably because around the same time three operas on this theme had appeared, one of which, with a libretto by Bertati, had been a fair success. There are certainly some resemblances between the two libretti, but they are confined to external structure and a few minor points of detail.

Mozart and da Ponte were both in Prague from the beginning of October to supervise the production and to complete the score, namely the parts (Masetto and the Commendatore) which were to be sung by Guiseppe Lolli whose vocal talents Mozart

Don Giovanni, autograph facsimile of a page from Act II, No. 25 (Paris, Bibliothéque du Conservatoire).

did not know. From the manuscript it can be seen that the overture to *Don Giovanni* was written in rather a hurry, although not, as legend has it, on the night before the premiere.

The Prague audiences at those first performances gave the opera a standing ovation comparable to that for *The Marriage of Figaro*, and the passage of time has done nothing to diminish its popularity.

The legend of Don Juan appears throughout European literature and popular folklore. This tale of vice and irreverence first found poetic and literal expression in Spain early in the 17th century in Tirsa de Mollina's *Burlador de Sevilla*.

The 18th century introduced into the traditional treatment of the legend didactic and moralizing overtones as exemplified by Goldoni's and Moliere's plays and by Gluck's ballet *Don Juan or the Libertine Punished*.

143

View of Prague.

The National Theater in Prague.

Title page of the *Prague* symphony.

Rarely had Mozart produced a score that was so replete with such rapid changes of mood, from tender love duets to grim outbursts of divine retribution.

Don Giovanni is the anti-hero of the opera and Leporello, his servant, incarnates many comic qualities and is an excellent contrast to his master. The anxieties of the two heroines, Donna Anna and Donna Elvira, are described with great feeling; and the Commendatore personifies the powers of heaven. These disparate qualities are fused by Mozart in a masterpiece which has been generally acknowledged as one of the greatest operas of all time.

Whereas in *The Marriage of Figaro* Mozart had to adapt Beaumarchais's masterpiece with its modern plot and characterisations, in *Don Giovanni* he had to handle more challenging material, an age-old legend that had not yet been given an adequate and credible embodiment on the operatic stage.

The period of Mozart's work on *Don Giovanni* saw a farreaching change in public mood. In the late 1780s the German and Austrian artistic and intellectual communities displayed a close interest in exploring philosophical, moral and ethical problems. Indeed, the idea of man's lofty mission, the meaning of human existence, the mysteries of love and death, the nature of human relationships, all these ran through some of the most outstanding dramatic and literary works of the period including Goethe's *Werther* and *Faust*, Heinse's *Ardinghello*, Schiller's *Don Carlos*. The freedom of the individual, and his right to personal happiness were in the focus of public discussions at the time.

Essentially, these problems were the outward expression of a tight tangle of contradictory ideas and conceptions which arose in the course of struggle against outmoded rationalistic attitudes. At the same time attempts were being made to interpret in broad philosophical terms existing contradictions of human existence. The vigorous and spirited assertion of the sensual basis of human life and freedom of the individual was set against the lofty ideas of universal justice and submission to moral duty.

This conflict was reflected with great poetic power in two masterpieces, one musical, the other literary, from the pen of two geniuses. They were Mozart's *Don Giovanni* and Goethe's *Faust* (fragments from the latter first appeared in 1790). The opposition of man's moral duty and his sensual nature is treated by both in terms of recognition of their unity in conflict. The ideas that agitated the minds of Mozart's contemporaries formed the basis of his musical conception and determined his approach to working out the imagery he was going to use in *Don Giovanni*. In the light of these ideas the relationships among the characters, including the minor and episodic ones, became involved directly in the same dramatic conflict. As a result a comic plot which many at the time saw as crude and banal, unexpectedly, in Mozart's interpretation, took on an almost tragic dimension.

Displaying remarkable boldness Mozart used a long familiar, almost banal, outline to create a completely new dramatic work.

Mozart draws the opera's characters proceeding from his own, often contradictory, ideas. The central character, Don Giovanni, goes far beyond the traditional framework of a comedy character. In his characterisation of Don Giovanni Mozart emphasises his power, his extraordinary charm and indomitable will. The whole of Don Giovanni's part, down to his smallest remarks, is instinct with a noble and courageous spirit, for all the outward carefree unconcern, and scintillating gaiety. Far from being a comic lover, Don Giovanni is a powerful personality, fateful in his charisma and quite a match for the Commendatore.

Even in Leporello's arias and remarks Mozart emphasises those features which for all their genuine comic character still

Vienna, the Stock in
Eisen Square and St.
Stephen's Cathedral.
Colored engraving by
Karl Schütz, 1779.

reflect the charm radiated by his master. Thus in Leporello's famous aria "Here is a List I Would Show You" in which he lists his master's conquests, the first part reflects the comic in Leporello, while the second, with its soft, caressing and at the same time masterful melody, elevates the aria associating it with the character of Don Giovanni. By uniting the serious and the comic Mozart throws the opera's characters into bold relief.

Mozart the dramatist has been compared, with some justice, with Shakespeare whose works he knew well. Like Shakespeare, Mozart made bold use of picaresque scenes to emphasize the tragic dimension of situations. Like Shakespeare, Mozart lends his characters tremendous emotional power and fills his thought with concentrated dramaticism. And like Shakespeare, by making his characters generalised in broad philosophical terms Mozart ensured their enduring appeal for future generations. Don Giovanni's indomitable courage, the cowardice of

Leporello, the poetic inner world of Donna Anna, the reckless and noble self-sacrifice of Elvira and the charming guile and simple-heartedness of Zerlina later found reflection in an infinite number of musical and literary works.

Whereas *Figaro* might be described as a comedy of characters *Don Giovanni* shows the unmistakable features of a new operatic form—psychological drama. Mozart was aware that his treatment and interpretation went beyond the framework of existing genre classification. He could not very well call *Don Giovanni* either *opera seria* or *opera buffa*, instead he settled on "*dramma giocosa*", i.e. "comic drama" thereby emphasizing the equality of its tragic and comic elements.

In *Don Giovanni* Mozart boldly ventured to do what he had studiously avoided in *Figaro*. Following the general lyrical trend in *Figaro* he was prepared to sacrifice the character nature of some of the heroes. In *Don Giovanni*, on the contrary, he was attracted by the idea of comparing heterogeneous elements. Exalted and picaresque characters, lyricism and grotesque are present in contrasting juxtaposition throughout the opera. *Don Giovanni* which marked a new and final phase in the evolution of Mozart's dramatic art, when it reached its acme, is dominated not by a lyrical atmosphere as its unifying principle which can easily be upset by the intrusion of a foreign element, but by a clearly-defined musical and dramatic idea which organises all the constituent elements into a powerful integrated whole and becomes most apparent in contrasting comparisons and juxtapositions.

The utmost clarity of the opera's dominant idea determined the simple logic of its structure: two contrasted characters— Don Giovanni and the Commendatore, run through the whole opera developing in clashes and confrontation with each other in successive settings of escalating tension. The purpose-oriented dynamism of its development sets *Don Giovanni* apart from Mozart's earlier operas in that it confers on theatrical music a degree of effectiveness and dramaticism of message which subsequently would be attained by Beethoven in his sonatas and symphonies.

The Commendatore is portrayed by methods which have more to do with instrumental music than with vocal. His characterisation is largely concentrated in the orchestra while its vocal basis is a measured recitative, a monotonous repetition of one and the same sound which in the finale makes this part sound like church music. This resemblance lends the image of the statue of the Commendatore a mysterious coloring devoid of recognisable earthly features.

By contrast, Don Giovanni's part emphasizes these very features. His arias, remarks and his parts in the ensembles are characterised by a song-and-dance style with elements of minuet and march clearly predominating as evidenced by the middle part of Leporello's aria "Here is a List I Would Show You" which is minuet-based and by the duet "Give me your Hand, Zerlina" which is vaguely based on a march.

By developing these contrasting musical elements in the parts of the other characters, Mozart achieves complete and well-rounded imagery.

First version of the libretto of *Don Giovanni* printed in Vienna for the first performance in Prague. This was replaced by another version adapted by Da Ponte.

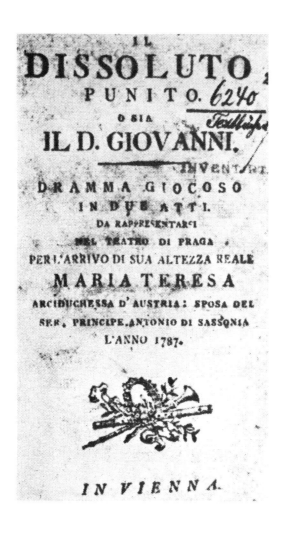

IL DISSOLUTO PUNITO. O SIA IL D. GIOVANNI. DRAMMA GIOCOSO IN DUE ATTI. DA RAPPRESENTARSI NEL TEATRO DI PRAGA PER L'ARRIVO DI SUA ALTEZZA REALE MARIA TERESA ARCIDUCHESSA D'AUSTRIA: SPOSA DEL SER. PRINCIPE ANTONIO DI SASSONIA L'ANNO 1787. IN VIENNA.

In *Don Giovanni*, more than in any of his earlier works, Mozart sought to achieve maximum full-bloodedness and adequacy of its musical media of expression, to develop fully complete forms which alone could bring out the philosophical message of his material. In each aria Mozart sought to disclose its intrinsic image, the essence of his hero, rather than highlight an individual character trait. A good example of this is Don Giovanni's famous aria "I'm in the mood for laughter and wine" which reveals the charismatic power and drive of his character. The ensembles in *Don Giovanni* are used by Mozart to describe conflict-dominated psychological moments, or else a particular mood that envelops all the characters involved in a scene. Mozart creates such mood-dominated psychological ensembles by combining the devices he used in the dramatic ensembles of *Idomeneo* and in the comic ensembles of *Die Entfuhrung* and *Fi-*

garo. In *Don Giovanni* Mozart is at his brilliant best in blending high dramaticism and romantic heroics with the simplicity, freedom and natural flow of musical speech.

Don Giovanni's ensembles came as a convincing refutation of the thesis that the completeness of certain operatic forms upset the natural development of the action, inhibited and fragmentized the movement of events. This thesis dominated composers' thinking for a long time. Indeed, Mozart's great contemporary Gluck, and later Wagner, as they developed their theory of musical drama, sought to work out new vocal forms and new techniques of scenic development, designed to replace the conventional methods of expressing human emotions that had been predominant in the musical theatre. Their arguments seemed convincing and to many beyond dispute. Indeed, while one could equate the aria with theatrical monologue, and justify operatic love duets where the slowing down of the action and the resulting brief "pause" might be seen as a natural embodiment of the psychological state of the heroes, how could one justify the scenic function of large ensembles in which several characters at a time either pour their hearts out or explain their intentions or actions? To a composer guided by the laws of the drama theatre this clearly contradicted artistic verity and, indeed, common sense itself.

Program of the first performance of *Don Giovanni* in Prague.

After a long period of radical attempts to avoid complete ensemble structures operatic composers inevitably came full circle and created some of their best music in this form. Witness the ensembles of Mozart, Verdi, and Rossini whose right to existence in the musical theatre is not challenged by anyone.

Mozart was prepared to agree with Gluck that music lacks a concrete and tangible message of the kind that the spoken word

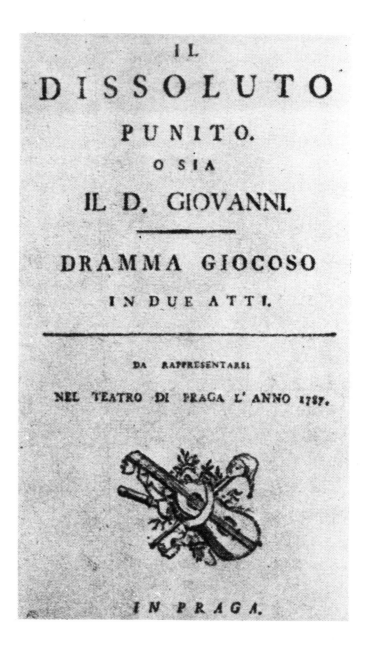

Title page of the libretto of *Don Giovanni* printed in Prague. This final version was used at the first performance of this work.

has and for this reason cannot claim the leading role in the development of the external theatrical action. But Mozart knew that in the area of human emotions and psychological states music was more expressive and effective than any words. And whenever he felt the need to emphasize this point Mozart boldly accepted a certain disparity between music and drama. In some cases he even sacrificed ordinary scenic verisimilitude in order to bring out the supreme dramatic truth, as he saw it, by employing purely musical means of expression. It was this independent development of his musical thought that discerning members of the audience were quick to appreciate and respond to.

A good example of this in *Don Giovanni* is the *terzetto* following the duel scene in the *Introduzione*: the fatally wounded Commendatore falls while Don Giovanni and Leporello stand over his body in consternation. This treatment of the scene is entirely Mozart's. Other Italian composers before him had treated it in a theatrically straightforward and more life-like way. In Gazzaniga's opera *Don Giovanni* fatally wounds the Commendatore and after snuffing out the candle with the tip of his sword quickly disappears together with Leporello. Everything happens in a flash.

Playbill for the first Viennese performance of *Don Giovanni*, 7 May 1788.

By contrast, Mozart in this tragic scene slows down the action. In his treatment the external dynamism of the scene recedes to the background under the impact of the musical and lyric-philosophical foreground: three low male voices come together in a theme which is more instrumental than vocal in character, to create a mood at once sombre and strangely radiant. The orchestral accompaniment with its measured rhythmic triplets also employs, to great effect, the low soft timbre of the cellos. Incidentally, Beethoven was said to have entered in his memorandum book an outline of this accompaniment and later noted down beside it the first movement of his *Moonlight Sonata* which recalls the melody, the harmonisation of the orchestral accompaniment and the overall mood of Mozart's *terzetto*.

Thus, Mozart emphasizes the moment of the Commendatore's death by a lyrical digression forming part of the noisy movement of the opera. The unexpected contrast between the terzetto's dramatic tone and the almost *buffo* character of the preceding material and the contemplative philosophical coloring of the whole scene combined to communicate to the audience Mozart's dramatic subtext: by killing the Commendatore Don Giovanni committed a crime against human morality.

Mozart and his librettist da Ponte turned Bertati's one-act libretto into their own great two-act *opera buffa*. In Bertati, the cemetery scene and the nocturnal feast, and Don Giovanni's death follow immediately after the rescue of Zerlina from the clutches of her seducer by Donna Elvira. The grand Finale of the first act was of da Ponte's own invention; he also doubled the length of the second act by adding, rather clumsily, a series of trivialities and dramatic postponements. But for Mozart they were not clumsy expedients. Without them we would never have heard the wonderful Trio in A major, Don Giovanni's famous Serenade, or the great Sextet, in which so much of grief and dignity finds expression in music. Mozart would offset dramatic weaknesses in the libretto with an overflow of pure nonfunctional beauty, seeming to ask the audience to stay a while. At such moments the semblance of reality no longer matters. It all becomes openly play-acting. For this is opera and in opera Mozart followed his maxim that "poetry should be music's obedient daughter".

The question of tempo in *Don Giovanni*'s two Finales, which are marvels of rapidity, is one of reconciling music and action, to which there are several solutions. In the *opera seria* it is as simple as in Wagner's music-drama. In the former there is a clear division between the aria, in which the music lingers, and the *recitativo secco*, in which it is pushed forward. And Wagner uses a symphonic orchestra under cover of which voices can declaim as rapidly as desired. In *Don Giovanni* Mozart found the golden mean, rare indeed in opera. His *Introduzione* is one of the acknowledged wonders of the world: Leporello's remarks, as he walks back and forth under Donna Anna's window, on the passionate duet between seducer and victim, the Commendatore's entry, the duel and its tragic end. And then, immediately, the whisper of the *recitativo secco*, and Donna Anna's cry when she returns. It is just right: not a spare bar nor yet a bar too few. Were *Don Giovanni* a play the director would have to choose the tempi; in the opera, Mozart's are so perfect that dramatic and musical needs are both completely satisfied. It is not just brevity; it is that despite its brevity it is so complete. In the Second Finale this quality increases to an almost explosive pitch both in Elvira's last attempt to rescue Don Giovanni and in the fateful D minor passage when the Commendatore pronounces the judgement of heaven which has been generally regarded as the acme of dramatic force.

Death of the Commendatore, a scene from *Don Giovanni*. From an engraving by J.H. Rumberg, 1825.

Don Giovanni was premiered in Prague on 29 October, 1787. The singers, except for the talented Luigi Bassi who took the part of Don Giovanni, were mediocre but with experience and a good sense of the musical theatre. Bondini's theatre lacked funds and for this reason there were not enough actors for all the roles. Thus the central tragic part of the Commendatore and the secondary *buffo* part of Masetto were taken by one and the same actor. As always, Mozart got on well with the actors: they understood him well and followed his directions without argument. Mozart insisted on maximum naturalness of intonation, gesture and attitude.

Mozart's two visits to Prague, early in the year when he received the commission for *Don Giovanni* from Bondini and in the autumn, when the opera was performed, seemed to him like one sweet dream: *Le Nozze di Figaro* had been a huge success in Prague to become a favourite with the public. Quadrilles to tunes from *Figaro* were danced at every ball in the city, the violin players in every coffee house did arias from *Figaro*. The Prague public gave an equally warm reception to *Don Giovanni*. Mozart's concerts were brilliantly successful too and were held amid wide publicity. In Prague with its ancient musical culture and a discerning public whose Slavic big-heartedness and gentle manner appealed to Mozart, he was both loved and understood.

Returning to Vienna after his "festival" in Prague was a painful experience for Mozart. For Vienna where he spent the ten most productive years of his life and where he had troops of friends and colleagues did not give him the sort of professional support and appreciation that was his due. The only "silver lining" was his close friendship with Joseph Haydn.

Second-rate mediocre composers whom no one cares to remember today received subsidies and grants from the court. Mozart was denied this royal favour. True, in 1788, the Emperor at long last, offered him the post of *Kammerkompositeur* (Court-Composer) that fell vacant on Gluck's death. His duties were to compose only music for "pleasure festivals" and masked balls at Schonbrunn Palace for a yearly salary of 800 florins, a beggar's dole. Mozart commented bitterly: "Too much for what I do; too little for what I could do."

After the first Vienna performance of *Don Giovanni* on 7 May, 1778, which did not please the Emperor* Mozart pro-

---

*According to da Ponte, the emperor said: "The opera is divine, possibly finer even than 'Figaro', but it is hardly the meat for my Viennese." When the comment was reported to Mozart he replied: "We shall have to give them time to chew it."

Top:
Silhouette of Anna Selina
(Nancy) Storace
(1766-1817), the first
Susanna in *Figaro*. She
was a noted English
soprano of Italian origin.

Bottom:
Silhouette of Michael
Kelly as Busilio in
Figaro.

duced in quick succession three of his best symphonies: in E-flat major, in G minor and in C major. After a period of frenetic work in the symphonic form in Salzburg (which resulted in over 35 symphonies) he returned to the symphony but rarely. In fact, Mozart was fully absorbed in writing operas and produced only one symphony, in D major, apparently for his Prague concerts in the year which saw the appearance of *The Marriage of Figaro*. After *Don Giovanni* which capped everything Mozart had sought to say in his earlier operas his interest in the symphony awakened. The three symphonies he wrote on the heels of *Don Giovanni* show just how far he had advanced not only from the orchestral thinking of his youth but also from the symphonic masterpieces of his Viennese predecessor and teacher, Joseph Haydn.

Whereas most of Mozart's previous symphonies were largely in the category of musical entertainment, a popular form with Salzburg and Viennese composers, his last three symphonies are full-scale dramatic works with a profound message, and featuring specific, highly individual structure and musical idiom.

Using a dramatic type of melody of his own invention which in terms of intonational diversity approximates to human speech, Mozart provides vivid musical images already in the opening themes of the three symphonies. Their structure is far more broadly based than any of Haydn's thematic structures, and at the same time their expressiveness and emotional appeal immediately recall Mozart's operatic images. Evidence of this is provided by the theme of the G minor symphony which is clearly related to one of Mozart's favourite operatic characters, Cherubino (*Figaro*). This relation is apparent both in the common rhythmical structure of the theme with Cherubino's aria "*I will tell you and explain*" and equally in its impetuous, excited intonation which conveys a poetic sense of life's movement. This is an instrumental embodiment of romantic youth, an image that attracted Mozart in the opera so much.

Individualization of the theme affected the message and structure of the symphony as a whole. In it Mozart achieved what none of his predecessors could, namely, an organic unity of the cycle. Haydn in his time had taken the first step in this direction: by abandoning heroic intonations in the first movement of his symphonies he brought them closer to genre music (domestic musical entertainment). Mozart took a different approach. He subordinated all the movements of a symphony to the initial, dominant image: in the G minor symphony he dramatises not only the first two movements but also the Minuet and the Finale which had ordinarily been treated in the manner of domestic musical entertainment. The Minuet loses its gallant

Silhouettes of Haydn, Gluck, Mozart and Salieri, engraved by H. Löschenkohl for the *Osterreichischer Nationalkalender* of 1786.

Haydn

Gluck

Mozart

Salieri

features to take on austere and dignified overtones. The Finale introduces active, dramatically significant intonations instead of playful, song-and-dance elements. The excited character of the opening theme seems to permeate every movement of the symphony and the Finale, despite a suggestion of "motor" tempo, does not defuse this sense of excitement. If anything, it adds to the musical tension.

The symphony has no introduction rather uncharacteristically of Mozart. The theme is introduced suddenly without warning, as if articulated on impulse, in one sustained breath, as it were. This dynamic directness is typical of the beginning of the more spectacular arias written by Mozart (Cherubino, Elvira). In terms of its expressiveness the G minor symphony prefigured romantic musical thinking and formed the basis for the symphonic creativity of Schubert, Schuman and many other composers.

Beside the G minor symphony, the E-flat major symphony seems, at first glance, less innovative and more like symphonic musical entertainment in the Haydn mould. This impression is created by the dance-like character of its thematic material, its closeness to everyday imagery. The latter, however, from the opening bars of the symphony takes on a poetic coloring, so characteristic of Mozart, and this sets the symphony apart from the composer's previous symphonic output. A grand dramatic introduction bearing the stamp of Mozart's operatic genius, a solemn march and passionate intonations contrast with the sub-

The final two pages of Mozart's thematic *Catalogue of all my works,* begun in 1784. The last entries are for *The Magic Flute, La Clemenza di Tito,* the Clarinet Concerto in A major and the Masonic Cantata, K.623 (Vienna, Österreiche Nationalbibliothek).

sequent exposition of the material. Other themes of the symphony are poetic, featuring considerable intonational diversity. Incidentally, the contrast between the solemn opening and the mundane character of the rest of the symphony was a favourite device with Mozart which he used in his earlier works as well. After the appearance of the symphony in E-flat major this device was warmly acclaimed by Haydn who, after Mozart's death, used it in his celebrated London symphonies.

One of the more popular movements of this symphony, it proved later, was the Minuet, apparently thanks to the new features which Mozart introduced into his treatment of this highly popular 18th-century dance.

Mozart's manuscript of the symphony in G minor, 3rd movement, minuet.

160

The opening page of Mozart's last symphony, the "Jupiter". The manuscript, originally in the Preussische Staatsbibliothek, Berlin, disappeared in 1945. A reproduction, however, had already been published in 1923.

In an attempt to move away from the elegant minuet of the rococo era, Haydn turned to the folk dance with its robust, if coarse, humour. Mozart, by contrast, lent the minuet a suggestion of chivalry, courage and *eclat*. Mozart's minuet seems to be stamped with that sense of imperiousness, and charismatic heroics which were so much in evidence in the character of Don Giovanni.

Mozart gave particular attention to the second, slow movement whose contemplative and dreamy character seems to reflect Mozart's own lyrical philosophy.

Mozart's last symphony in C major, better known as the "Jupiter" Symphony owing to its grand scale, is the biggest of his triad of great symphonies of 1788 and the most complex in form and structure. The "Jupiter" Symphony is a remarkable masterpiece for its perfection and innovations which anticipated Beethoven's symphonism. The symphony's material is replete with sharp contrasts. The main movement contains two elements—short gamut-like upward flights of sound, with their heroic and insistent "clarion call" and a lyrical, evasive response, with its soft and elegiac tone. This contrast is developed throughout the rest of the symphony—the second theme arises out of the elegiac element of the main theme. This profoundly lyrical image is developed later in the second movement. The stark contrast of the two themes is accentuated further by the intrusion of an ordinary folk melody in the concluding part of the first movement; an ordinary, undramatised Minuet is followed by a broadly-designed heroic Finale noted for its intricate complexity of form and thematic material. In it Mozart brings together elements of the fugue and the sonata, the two principal forms of 18th-century music.

Frontispiece title of the score of symphony in E-flat, edition published in 1797 by André of Offenbach.

The three symphonies are characterised by a combination of an exalted, lofty philosophical message and ordinary, mundane elements. This combination also runs through Mozart's operatic output and would later find even more vivid expression in Beethoven's symphonies which share many of the features of Mozart's work.

In all three symphonies Mozart employs the classical composition of orchestra as established by Haydn including the same timbre comparisons between different groups of instruments. But unlike Haydn, Mozart uses the timbre range of the solo instruments in a more individualised way. This lends Mozart's scores a more refined character and brings them very close to the expressiveness of his vocal music.

Mozart's triad of great symphonies of 1788 exerted a tremendous influence on the evolution of the symphony in all of West-European music.

Die Zauberflöte (The Magic Flute)

Mozart tackled his last opera, *The Magic Flute*, with all the resources of his extraordinary skill when writing vocal and symphonic music. He wrote it in 1791, finishing it shortly before his death. The previous two years had been particularly hard for the Mozart family: a relentless but inadequately diagnosed illness was sapping his strength, and his financial position, it seemed, had never been so desperate. This was the time of the desperate begging letters to Michael Puchberg, a merchant well-disposed towards him. These letters continued until Mozart's death. In April 1789, the composer, in desperation, went to Berlin on a concert engagement. The young Prince Karl Lichnowsky gave him a seat in his coach. Mozart performed in the presence of King Friedrich Wilhelm II, a middling cellist and a great music-lover; but the trip brought him nothing except a present of a hundred Friedrichsdors and a commission for six quartets and as many sonatas for the King's eldest daughter. A few days after his return, Mozart was again writing to Puchberg: "God, I am in such straits as I would not wish on my worst enemy." In the autumn of 1789, after a revival of *The Marriage of Figaro* on the Viennese stage, Mozart nevertheless managed to obtain a commission for an opera. This was the Italian-style *opera buffa Cosi fan tutte*, again written in collaboration with da Ponte. The premiere took place in January 1790 and was moderately well received. In the opinion of the Viennese, it could not compare with *Figaro*.

Mozart was being dogged by bad luck all this time. He was not invited to the coronation of Leopold II in Frankfurt, and a

Prince Carl Lichnowsky
(1756-1814). Oil-painting,
anonymous
(Czechoslovakia, Schloss
Hradec).

Manuscript from the opera *Cosi fan Tutte*.

journey that he undertook at his own expense proved fruitless: he did not succeed in making a single public appearance. A month before, he had written an opera *La Clemenza di Tito* to a libretto by Metastasio in the spirit of the Italian *opera seria*. It was commissioned by Prague to be performed for the coronation of King Leopold II of Bohemia. Mozart's opera was simple, mature and sublime; but the coronation public found it boring.

Mozart did not lose heart, fighting his terrible illness with all the powers at his command and remaining as open and trusting as always in his relations with other people. More than ever before, he felt the need to be surrounded by people from the world of art and was always glad of a jest or a few carefree moments. During these difficult times, one of his oldest Salzburg friends, the impresario Schikaneder, persuaded him to write for the popular stage a German national opera with magic as its theme. Mozart agreed, partly to rescue Schikaneder who was anxious for something new to revitalise his theatre in a suburb of Vienna, although he did not have the money to pay for the commission. And so *The Magic Flute* came into being, one of the most remarkable works of art ever written and the beginning of romantic opera.

The libretto was hastily written by Schikaneder himself. The plot was taken from Wieland's popular verse fairy-tale "Lulu", but was then subjected to such unforeseen changes that it was hard to find any traces of Wieland's poem in it. It may be that Schikaneder himself insisted on the changes, since a show based on a very similar plot was running at a neighbouring theatre, and the experienced impresario decided to rehash the libretto on the spot. Either way, the former negative characters suddenly became positive and all the situations were turned inside out. The light fairy-tale plot, however, justified any kind of perversion, and subsequently Goethe, on reading the libretto of *The Magic Flute*, affirmed that nothing could be better as a scenario for a magic opera.

Mozart was attracted by Schikaneder's scheme for two reasons: first, he was again dealing with German national opera and he could carry out his long-cherished intentions, but this time armed with the skill of maturity; secondly, the plot of *The Magic Flute* and the libretto itself gave him *carte blanche* to build up his own musical and dramatic conception and Mozart had always found this attractive.

In unity of concept, scope of thematic development and philosophical treatment of the characters and human relationships, *The Magic Flute* may be considered a worthy rival to *Don Giovanni*. It is, however, certainly not a psychological drama, but

165

a fairy-tale opera, closely bound up with the comedy traditions of the Austrian musical theatre, the Viennese *Singspiel*. Also borrowed from *Singspiel* is the structure of the scenes in which the arias alternate with dialogue and, even more important, the local colour, which is clearly expressed in the music, the stage characters and the overall tone of the presentation.

It is characteristic that Mozart here too should have introduced elements of the philosophical problems with which his intimate friends were concerned. In this case, there are unmistakeable echoes of Masonic ideas that have been woven into the fairy-tale plot.

In the second half of the 1780s, Mozart began taking a direct part in the activity of the Austrian Freemasons, a society with very vague aims and objectives, but representing to some extent the progressive forces in society. Mozart's friends were members of various Viennese lodges and they introduced him to their organisation.

Mozart took his Freemasonry with the seriousness that was typical of him in anything to do with intellectual life. He was attracted by the humanist ideas of fraternity and love which were being preached in the Masonic lodges. He is unlikely to have been aware of the backstage political activities of most of the lodges, and so he idealised the Masons, calling them "the best people." He subsequently introduced his father and even Haydn to his own lodge. Several wonderful cantatas, written for

Title page of the piano score of Mozart's *Der Schauspiel-Direktor*. This comic *Singspiel* was commissioned by Emperor Joseph II and was presented at Schonbruun in 1786.

Program for the Vienna premiere of *The Magic Flute*.

Die Zauberflöte.

Eine

große Oper in zwey Aufzügen.

Von

Emmanuel Schikaneder.

———

Die Musik ist von Herrn Wolfgang Amade
Mozart, Kapellmeister, und wirklichem k.
k. Kammer = Compositeur.

Wien,
gedruckt bey Ignaz Alberti. 1791.

Title page of the libretto of *The Magic Flute*.

ceremonial occasions, testify to his attendance at Masonic gatherings.

Mozart suffered two grievous losses in the last years of his life: the death of his father, whom he loved deeply and with great devotion, and the death of one of his best friends, Ignaz von Born, a nobleman and master of a Masonic lodge. This intensified Mozart's philosophical mood, the more so as after the death of Joseph II, the Masons fell on hard times. Austria's new monarch was unfavourably disposed towards the lodges and regarded the members as "progeny of revolution", destroyers of order and religion. Social and philosophical problems and Masonic symbolism, in a private, very original and lively interpretation, lay behind the conception of *The Magic Flute*. The wise Sarastro with his strong-willed, stern attitude to life (evidently very closely associated with the personality of Ignaz von Born), the theme of the ordeals through which the young lovers must pass before they can be considered worthy of happiness, the very idea of the inevitable victory of light over the dark forces of evil and destruction (also more likely to have been inspired by von Born, to whom Mozart mentioned his intention, than by the need to break free of the presentation in the neighbouring

Mozart's Masonic Funeral Music in C minor, K.477. Autograph facsimile, November 1785 (Tübingen, Universitätsbibliothek).

theatre)—all this was the artistic realisation of thoughts and experiences inspired in Mozart by his Freemasonry.

But philosophical subjects did not tempt the composer into overloading his light comedy plot; he left unchanged the magic content and the characterisation of the principles. Lyrical elements predominate throughout the opera, and even in the tragic situations, such as the death of the Queen of the Night or Pamina's attempted suicide, Mozart never for one moment forgets that he is telling a fairy-tale, giving it a naive and slightly ironic treatment. In this, more than in anything else, Mozart's innate and remarkable feeling for style is in evidence, together with his individual approach to the plot and its dramatic possibilities.

It was the national fairy-tale style that was new in Mozart's work and gave *The Magic Flute* its uniqueness and originality. A decisive role was played in his design by folk-poetry ideas as they occurred in the Austrian popular tradition. This applies above all to the turbulent, spontaneous feelings of the characters—love at first sight and hatred that vanishes no less suddenly. Hence the good-natured touch of parody, and the light, carefree and sometimes coarse humour that is woven into even the most serious episodes.

The characters in *The Magic Flute* are remarkably varied, not only in their closeness to the world of fairy-tale, to which some of them obviously belong: the Queen of the Night, for example, and Papageno. But with them are characters portrayed with psychological realism rather than fantasy, such as Tamino and Pamina. Mozart gave these lyrical personages more detailed and dramatic musical portraits and a subtly psychological musical interpretation.

Very special and completely new to the operatic stage is Sarastro, the romantic image of a philanthropic sage, who subsequently took up an honourable place in fairy-tale opera writing, with variations according to the plot. He is the personification of the lofty spiritual principle of life which is contrasted in the fairy-tale with human passions and failings. It is typical that Mozart, when creating the image of Sarastro, should have come nearer to folk song in the musical interpretation of the part than for any of the other characters.

The hints of parody in Mozart's musical characterisation are also entirely new and varied, from the naive, zestful humour in the portrayal of the fantastic Papageno, half-man, half-bird, to the subtly caustic parody in the part of the Queen of the Night. This malignant and vengeful character is portrayed by means of extremely difficult Italian-style coloratura arias. The coloratura element gives a touch of humour to her turbulent passions; the intentionally high *tessitura*, the repetitions of the staccato vocal passages, the duel between voice and flute—all these traditional techniques of the aria of revenge acquire a suggestion of parody in *The Magic Flute*.

It may be that, apart from his philosophical notions of good and evil, Mozart was also inspired by a purely topical aim—to portray the positive heroes through the national music and the negative ones through Italian. In any case, the Queen of the Night is presented as a typical Italian operatic prima donna. In spite of his long-standing attachment to Italian opera, Mozart could not look with indifference on the low prestige of his native art and could not help dreaming that the Italian and Austrian theatres should change places. Mozart may have had a definite aim in mind when applying this technique to his opera.

In spite of the hybrid structure of the plot, the blend of fantastic and realistic images and of comic and dramatic incidents, the musical development of *The Magic Flute* has grace, unity and logicality, sometimes even more tangibly than in Don Giovanni. This is all the more amazing, since the magic nature of the opera and the spoken dialogue revived the division of genre and national signs typical of *Il Seraglio*. Cheek by jowl again, yet not mixing with one another, we find the traditional *aria seria* and the *aria buffa*, the couplet song, the ballad, and a new type of dramatised lyrical monologue that finally crystallised out in Don Giovanni. Moreover, Mozart's national inclinations encouraged the idea of applying a totally new technique in opera: in portraying Sarastro's realm, he wove an ancient Protestant chorale into the fabric of the opera and, moreover, in the figurated arrangement typical of such chorales, he introduced Bach traditions straight into contemporary operatic music.

Nonetheless, Mozart subordinated all this heterogeneous material to a basic philosophical idea which, as in Don Giovanni, gave a firm foundation for his musical and dramatic intention. This was the idea of the ethical feat and the sublime purpose of love. It accounted for the appearance of the expressive themes of love, separation and the noble effect of art on the human soul (the "magic flute" theme). These expressive musical themes are developed throughout the opera, being repeated in certain situations and blending the heterogeneous elements into a whole. Many of them are given a symbolic meaning. In this way, the ground was being prepared for the system of leitmotifs that was to be so characteristic of the romantic opera.

As in *Don Giovanni*, so in *The Magic Flute* Mozart created a new kind of overture. The formulation of the dramatic idea in these operas led to the overture becoming wholly and specifically programmatic: the opening of the overture to Don Giovanni gives an instrumental exposition of the last meeting be-

Emanuel Schikaneder (1751-1812), German actor, playwright and theatrical manager. Apart from providing the libretto for *The Magic Flute*, he also worked with Beethoven.

Schikaneder in the rôle of Papageno at the first performance of *The Magic Flute*. Engraving, 1791.

A thematic list of some of Mozart's most popular works engraved by Preston of London in the 1790's or the early 1800's (Ates Orga).

between Don Giovanni and the Commendatore: the opening chords of the overture to *The Magic Flute* symbolise Sarastro's realm. The opening itself conveys the mysterious and fairy-tale atmosphere of this realm. At the same time, the symphonic development of both overtures acquires such independence and completion that they can be regarded as a specifically symphonic solution of the problems which the composer embodied in the operatic imagery.

Mozart, the last portrait.

The Requiem

The radiant poetry of *The Magic Flute* was one of Mozart's last achievements. By the time he finished the opera, the composer was already mortally ill. He worked on it at the same time as on the Requiem, the most tragic and philosophical of all his works. Both have gone down in history as a great artist's swan song. Mozart had long been oppressed by thoughts of ap-

173

Frontispiece of the first score of the *Requiem*, published in 1800.

proaching death; moreover, he was troubled by a strange circumstance associated with the commissioning of the *Requiem*. It was ordered by an unknown person in a dark cloak who asked him to finish the work by the appointed date at all costs; the payment arrived punctually at regular intervals, sent by the unknown person who refused to give his name. Mozart was in a great hurry to finish the *Requiem*; the plan of this work had troubled and attracted him for a long time. Often, with tears in his eyes, he said that he was writing it for himself. It was subsequently ascertained that the mysterious stranger was a servant of Count Walsegg zu Stuppach, a music-lover and amateur composer who quite frequently, without giving his name, commissioned works from established musicians and then passed them off in domestic concerts as his own. The count's wife had died some years previously; the mass which Mozart was writing was intended to honour the memory of the deceased, and the count, as on previous occasions, was going to pass off the Requiem as his own.

This wretched ruse cost the already harrassed Mozart some anxious moments. The stranger for whom he was writing the Mass troubled and oppressed his imagination. Nevertheless, he was composing his *Requiem* with the same inspiration that he usually felt when writing operas. This work was, indeed, close to his dramatic music in character: magnificent choruses and solo episodes corresponded least of all to the dogmatic themes of the church. This was an expression of real human feeling, a tragic premonition of death, of the unfathomable depths of human suffering, and yet also of the miraculous power of hope and love for humankind that permeated the whole of Mozart's work. Such movements as "Lacrimosa" show the insight of a genius into the secret recesses of the human soul.

In some musical respects, Mozart's *Requiem* is closely connected with the remarkable choral tradition of the German classical composers of the first half of the 18th century—such peaks as Bach's St. Matthew Passion and the Mass in B Minor, and also Handel's magnificent oratorios. Particularly close to them are such movements as the *Kyrie* ("Lord, have mercy"), written in the form of a double fugue on an austere theme in the old style. In *Dies Irae* (Day of Wrath), Mozart created a remarkable fantasy in the spirit of Handel's vivid choral passages: a vivid picture of the Last Judgement, in which a thunderous effect from the choir is intensified by the movement of the voices in unison, the blare of trombones, the solemn warning of the trumpets, an ominous tremolo on the strings and the rumbling of the tympani.

This sombre scene is contrasted with a totally different expression of grief: the tenor, contralto and soprano in the movements that follow convey the depths of human sorrow and, through a blend of courageous, illuminated and anguished states of soul, they lead up to the lyrical culmination of the whole work, the "Lacrimosa".

Mozart was unable to finish the *Requiem*. Certain parts remained unfinished, and only the *Requiem* and the Kyrie were written complete with vocal and orchestral parts. All the other movements were completed by Mozart's pupil, Franz Sussmayer, who never left Mozart's bedside during the composer's last days. Mozart had played the work through to him many times, explaining the means of handling this or that theme. In completing his teacher's work, Sussmayer added nothing of his own and simply carried out intentions as closely as possible to what he had heard and remembered of the composer's own rendering.

Mozart died during the night of 4 to 5 December 1791. A few hours before the end, he asked for a watch to be put by his pillow and in his mind he went through The Magic Flute, which was being performed that evening at Schikaneder's theatre. He listened with his inner ear for the last time to his beloved arias and ensembles.

None of his intimates was there when Mozart's remains were committed to the grave. None of his patrons, friends or acquaintances followed the coffin to the cemetery. His wife was gravely ill and in no state to leave her sick bed. On the day of the funeral, there was not even any small change in the house. Mozart was buried at St. Mark's cemetery in a pauper's grave. When his wife later tried to find it, she was unable to do so; the common graves were constantly being filled with corpses of those who had died in the cholera epidemic raging at the time. Even the sexton who had buried Mozart died shortly afterwards. Only he could have shown where the remains of the great composer had been interred.

So ended the life of one of the greatest geniuses the world has ever known. The true extent of Mozart's enormous legacy was not realised straightaway and by no means all his works have come down to posterity. Even so, their number and quality are simply staggering: seventeen operas, about fifty symphonies, an enormous number of instrumental works of various forms; long orchestral suites (serenades and divertimenti), many chamber compositions for various instrumental ensembles (particularly the string quartets dedicated to Haydn and the string quintets of the later years), virtuoso concertos for violin, piano, for wind instruments and orchestra, solo works for piano—sonatas, vari-

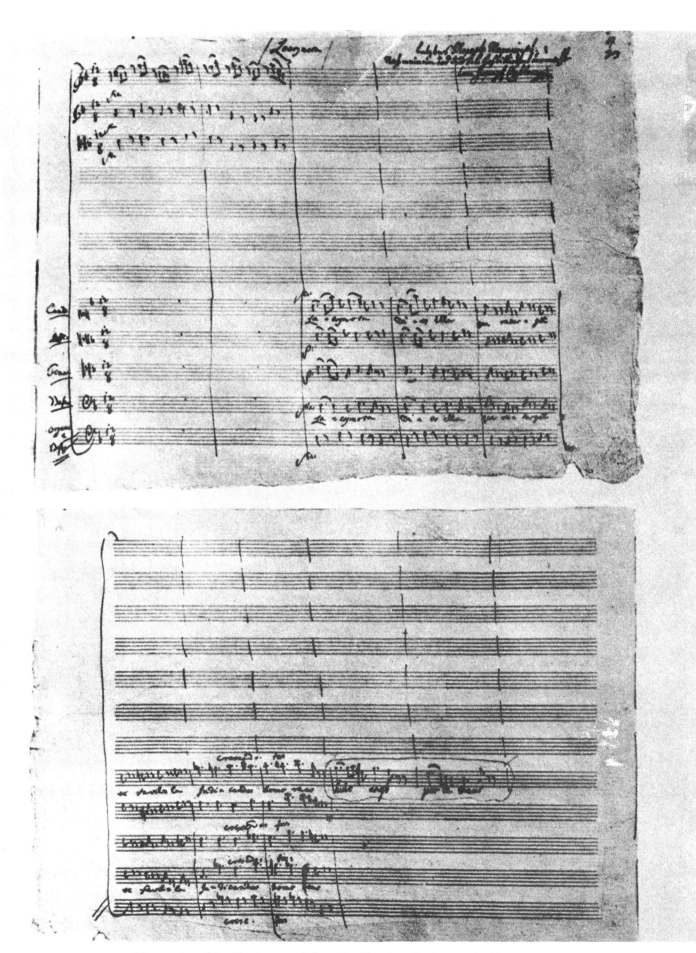

Manuscript of the "Lachrymosa" from the *Requiem,* the last music Mozart wrote.

The house where Mozart died.

The opening page of Mozart's String Quartet in D major, K.575, the first of the quartets written for the King of Prussia in June 1789: six were commissioned, only three were finished (London, British Museum).

ations, fantasias, rondos, fugues—, for the organ (the "church" sonatas), for mechanical instruments (the glass harmonica, the music-box). In addition to this incredibly long list, there are the major vocal and orchestral compositions: ecclesiastical (masses, litanies, offertories, hymns, motets) and secular oratorios and cantatas; then songs, concert arias and vocal ensembles. And all this was achieved in the course of a short lifetime.

Needless to say, not all these works are of equal merit: most of Mozart's childhood and some of his youthful compositions are only of interest to the research scholar who wishes to trace the origins and development of a genius. Only five operas of the mature period are still performed on the contemporary stage.

Poster for the last public concert in which Mozart participated, at Vienna in March 1791. He played his Concerto for piano and orchestra in B-flat that he had just completed in January of the same year (Mozart Museum, Salzburg).

Nachricht.

Herr Bähr, wirklicher Kammermusikus bey Sr. rußischen kaiserl. Majestät wird künftigen Freytag den 4. März die Ehre haben, im Saale bey Herrn Jahn sich in einer großen musikalischen Akademie zu verschiedenenmalen auf der Clarinette hören zu lassen; wobey Madame Lange singen, und Herr Kapellmeister Mozart ein Konzert auf dem Forte piano spielen wird. Diejenigen, so sich noch zu abboniren Belieben tragen, können täglich bey Herrn Jahn mit Billeten bedienet werden.

Der Anfang ist um 7 Uhr abends.

Of the fifty symphonies, some of the late ones, the summit of Mozart's symphonic art, are included in the contemporary concert repertoire. Certainly, Mozart's individuality and the meaning of his creative searchings are concentrated with particular intensity in these works: they are the culmination of his whole artistic career. But there are still many that are at present less accessible to the listener, since they are too seldom performed. They are awaiting revival and deserve to be equally longlived.

It is not easy to survey and evaluate all the aspects of Mozart's creative work at a glance: in many instrumental or vocal forms he achieved the heights of classical music in that era and at the same time went far ahead in terms of musical thought. The philosophical content of his symphonies, combined with the life-like precision of the images, already contained the seeds of Beethoven's powerful symphonies and anticipated the art of the Romantics. His innovations in opera, prevailing over the restrictions of rationalism, opened the way to a multifaceted and complex theatrical realism for composers all over the world. It is not surprising that the achievements of the genius who created the Austrian national opera should have awakened a response not only in works by masters of the European operatic stage who were relatively close to him in time—Cherubini, Rossini, Weber, and Auber, but also in those of the great 19th-century realists (particularly Glinka, Verdi, Bizet and Tchaikovsky), and in the bold innovators of our own century—Stravinsky, Prokofiev, Gershwin, Britten and others. And so every aspect of his musical art, every one of his works, is brought to ultimate perfection because of his rare genius, the severe demands he made upon himself and indefatigable, self-sacrificing toil.

Nevertheless, the myth of the carefree, divinely illuminated darling of fate, the myth of Mozart the wonder-composer has been current for a long time, overshadowing the true picture of his life and work. It was only dispelled thanks to the efforts of a veritable army of music scholars who devoted themselves to the study of Mozart's legacy. A contribution was also made by poets and writers who were able to fathom Mozart's creative in-

dividuality—Pushkin, Stendhal, Hoffman, Prosper Merimee and Romain Rolland. Much was also done by true music-lovers who carefully collected anything that could throw light on the real facts of Mozart's life and times: their shrewd assessments and informed guesses sometimes anticipated the research of the musicologists.

The first substantial biography of Mozart (published in 1829), which included much documentary material, testimonies, the reminiscences of people who knew Mozart intimately, his parents and friends (including the recollection of his sister Marianne, who survived him) was written by an official of the Danish Legation in Vienna, Georg Nikolaus von Nissen.* The first original research work dedicated not only to the composer's life but to an analysis of his work was done by a Russian music-lover, the Nizhni-Novgorod landowner A. I. Oulibischeff and published in 1843. Of outstanding importance was the compilation of a fully substantiated and systematised chronological catalogue of all Mozart's works; published in 1826, it was compiled by the Austrian botanist and mineralogist, Ludwig Kochel, a devoted admirer of the composer.

The systematic and in-depth study of Mozart's heritage by music scholars began in the second half of the 19th century in connection with the centenary of his birth and the publication of his complete works (1880-1905). Scholars from many countries took part, so that over a period of more than a hundred years there has been an accumulation of comprehensive multi-lingual *Mozartiana*, the study of which requires great expenditure of time and sustained effort, even by professional musicologists. It began with a compendious work (published in 1856) by the German musicologist Otto Jahn which laid the foundations for many subsequent research studies. Mozart's personality and career were presented somewhat one-sidedly: Jahn advocated classical lucidity in art, and in choosing Mozart as his model he created the idealised image of a balanced "sunny" artist. All that was tragic, turbulent, and philosophical in Mozart's work was circumvented and the contradictions were glossed over. Only gradually did these qualities, like the vast range of his searchings and achievements, win recognition in the works

---

*F. N. Nissen married Mozart's widow, Constanze, nine years after the composer's death and took on the responsibility of looking after his two sons (the younger subsequently became a distinguished pianist). He regarded the biography of Mozart as his life's work.

Mozart. Portrait in oils by Barbara Kraft, 1819 (Vienna, Gesellschaft der Musik-freunde). This was based on a detail from the family portrait of 1780-81 painted by Croce. According to Otto Erich Deutsch, Kraft worked under Nannerl's supervision: the picture 'appears to be the best and most faithful likeness of all.'

Constanze Mozart (1762-1842). Portrait by
Hans Hansen, 1802.

of 20th-century scholars: a remarkable work by Hermann Abert
(1921), a drastically revised version of the book by Otto Jahn;
a five-volume research work by the Polish scholar Theodore de
Wyzewa and the French musicologist Georges de Saint-Foix
(1912 and 1937-46), works by A. Heuss (1907), E. Dent (1913),
B. Paumgartner (1927), R. Haas (1933), the book by A. Einstein (1944), the Mozart biography by E. Schenk (1955). The
works of the Mozarteum (International Mozart Institution in
Salzburg), 1966, signalled a new stage in Mozart studies.

To this day, however, Mozart's work is still inadequately re-
searched, and contemporary generations of scholars and artists
still have much to do along these lines. It is a difficult task, but
an appealing one: in Mozart, the creator and the man, we see
the image of an artist, a humanist, strong-willed, with an in-
quiring mind, unshakeably in love with life, undismayed by its
contradictions, conscious of all the complexity and bitterness of
social relations among his contemporaries, but never losing his
passionate belief in the infinite goodness of the human soul.

Karl Thomas Mozart (1784-1858). Second and older surviving son of Wolfgang Amadeus and Constanze Mozart.

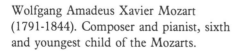

Wolfgang Amadeus Xavier Mozart (1791-1844). Composer and pianist, sixth and youngest child of the Mozarts.

Monument to Mozart in the cemetery where he was buried.

Selective Bibliography

1. *Letters: Die Briefe* W. A. Mozarts und seiner Familie, hrsg. von L. Schiedermayer, Bd 1-5, Munch.-Leipz. 1914; *Mozart W. A.* Briefwechsel und Aufzeichnungen, hrsg. von E. H. Müller von Asow, Bd 1-2, Lindau 1949; *Mozart W. A.* Briefe und Aufzeichnungen. Gesamtausgabe, hrsg. von der Internationalen Stiftung Mozarteum Salzburg. Gesammelt von W. A. Bauer und O. E. Deutsch. Auf Grund deren Vorarbeiten er utert von J. H. Eibl. Bd 1-7. Kassel, 1962-75.

2. *Fiction: Stendhal* (Beyle, Henri) "Vies de Haydn, de Mozart et de Metastase" 1817 (Oeuvres complètes, établ. du texte e pref. par H. Martineau, v. 1-79, Paris 1927-37).

   Hoffmann E.Th.A. "Don Juan", 1819 ("Fantasiestücke in Callot's Manier", Bd 1-4, 1814-15) Dichtungen und Schriften, Bd 1-15, Liechtenstein-Weimar, 1924.

   Rolland Romaine "Musicians d'autrefois" Paris, 1908.

   Morike Ed. "Mozart auf der Reise nach Prag", 1856 (Sämtliche Werke, Münch., 1964).

3. *Documentary Literature: Biancolli* L., The Mozart Handbook, N.Y., 1954; *Giasotto* R., Annali Mozartiani, Mil. 1956; *Deutsch*, O. E. Mozart. Die Dokumente seines Lebens. Kassel, 1961;

   Eibl, J. N. W. A. Mozart. Chronik seines Lebens. Lpz. 1965.

   Fischer H. C., Besch L., Das Leben Mozarts. Eine Dokumentation. Salzburg, 1968;

   Schlichtegroll F. V., Johannes Chrysostomus Wolfgang Gottlieb Mozart, Nekrolog auf das Jahr 1791, Gotha 1793;

   Niemtschek F. Leben des K. K. Kapellmeisters Wolfgang Gottlieb Mozart, nach Originalquellen beschrieben. Prag. 1798;

   Nissen G. N. v., Biographie W. A. Mozarts, Lpz. 1828;

   Oulibischeff A., Nouvelle biographie de Mozart, t. 1-3, Moscou, 1843;

   Fahn O., W. A. Mozart, Bd 1-4, Lpz. 1856-59;

   Heus A., Das dämonische Element in Mozarts Werken "ZJMG" 1906, Jahrg. 7, H. 5;

   Wyzewa Th. de, Saint-Fois G. de, W. A. Mozart, Sa vie musicale et son oeuvre de l'enfance à pleine maturité, t. 1-2, Paris 1912, suite-Saint-Fois G. de, W. A. Mozart, Sa vie musicale . . ., t 3-5, Paris 1937-46;

   Dent E., Mozart's operas, London, 1913, 1947;

   Lert E., Mozart auf dem Theater, Berlin, 1918;

   Abert H. W. A. Mozart. Neubearbeitete und erweiterte Ausgabe von Otto Jahns Mozart. Tl. 1-2. Lpz., 1919-21, 1955-56;

   Blumml E. K., Aus Mozarts Freundes-und Familiens-Kreis. Wien, 1923;

   Nettl P. W. A. Mozart, Frankf. Hamburg, 1955;

   Haas R. W. A. Mozart, Potsdam, 1933;

   Blom E., Mozart, London-N.Y., 1935;

   Kolb A., Mozart, Wien, 1937. 1956;

   Einstein A., Mozart, N.Y., 1945, neue Ausgabe: Mozart. Sein Charakter. Sein Werk, Frankf. 1968;

   Witold J., Mozart méconnu, Paris, 1954;

   Jacob H. E., Mozart oder Geist, Musik und Schicksal, Fr. 1955;

   Schenk E., W. A. Mozart, Z-Lpz-W., 1955;

   King A. H., Mozart in Retrospect, London, 1955, 1970;

   Greither A., Die sieben grossen Opern Mozarts. Versuche über das Verhältnis der Texte zur Musik, Heidelberg, 1956;

   Tchernaya. Mozart. His Life and Work, Moscow, 1956 (in Russian);

   Chicherin G., Mozart Issledovatelskii etyud. Leningrad. 1970, 1971;

   Bär C., Mozart, Krankheit, Tod, Begräbnis. Salzburg, 1966, 1972.

Index

Page numbers printed in **bold** refer to photographs or illustrations